A HALF-CENTURY OF FEDERAL RESERVE POLICYMAKING, 1914-1964

Clay J. Anderson
Economic Adviser

FEDERAL RESERVE BANK OF PHILADELPHIA

FOREWORD

November 16, 1964 marked the fiftieth anniversary of the Federal Reserve System. This half-century witnessed a transition in central bank policy from a simple, formalistic principle of using Bank Rate to influence the balance of payments and protect the gold reserve, to using central bank powers to achieve broad domestic economic goals as well as protect the external value of the currency.

Official records of policymaking discussions of Federal Reserve authorities have not been available to outside scholars and students of central banking. Recently a major step was taken in this direction: the minutes of the Federal Open Market Committee from 1936 to 1960 were made available to scholars at the libraries of the Board of Governors and the Reserve Banks, and the Library of Congress.

The primary purpose of this book is to bridge this gap; to make available a summary of the thinking of Federal Reserve officials about policy as it developed. The study is based almost entirely on the minutes of the meetings of the various policymaking bodies. The author's aim is an objective presentation of the principal views of the policymakers as they evolved in the course of a somewhat turbulent first fifty years.

Karl R. Bopp

May, 1965   *President*

iii

PREFACE

This book is a history of the central banking thought of Federal Reserve officials during the first half-century of the Federal Reserve System. The primary objective is to trace their thinking as they developed policies to meet the major problems arising from an ever-changing environment. What goals did policymakers try to achieve; what were their views as to the nature and causes of business fluctuations; what guides were considered useful in deciding when and what action should be taken to achieve these goals; how could the tools of Federal Reserve policy best be used and coordinated; how were policymakers influenced by a changing economic environment? These are some of the threads of thought the study tries to trace during fifty years of policymaking by Federal Reserve officials.

The author's aim is to present as objectively as possible the principal views on policy as expressed by policymakers themselves. There is no attempt to give the views of each official who participated, to discuss or appraise the role of individuals, or to evaluate policies formulated except for some of the author's views on the first fifty years given in the last chapter. The study is a history of ideas about policy rather than of policies actually pursued. Ideas did not come in a steady flow; they came in waves as Federal Reserve officials grappled with problems created by a somewhat turbulent environment.

The scope of the study is limited; it is based primarily on the views of officials as recorded in the minutes and proceedings of meetings of policymaking groups such as the Federal Open Market Committee and its predecessor committees; the Conference of Presidents (prior to August, 1935, the Governors of the Federal Reserve Banks); the Conference of Chairmen and Federal Reserve Agents of the Federal Reserve Banks prior to August, 1935; joint conferences of these groups with the Board of Governors (prior to August, 1935, the Federal Reserve Board), and the Board of Governors for selected periods. The detail with which discussion and views were recorded over the years varied widely. Although other sources were consulted at times, such as the Annual Reports of the Board of Governors and statements of Federal Reserve officials in Congressional hearings on the Federal Reserve System, the book is confined almost entirely to the minutes. They are the primary source of information on what officials were trying to do and why, and thus far most of this material is not available to the public.[1]

*	*	*

The author incurred many obligations in this study. Officials of the Federal Reserve Bank of Philadelphia, the Federal Reserve Bank of New York, and the Board of Governors made available minutes of policymaking conferences. The library staff of the Federal Reserve Bank of Philadelphia rendered valuable research assistance, including preparation of the list of policymakers given in the Appendix. The Secretary's office of the Board of Governors and librarians of some of the Reserve Banks cooperated willingly in checking and providing some of the information in the Appendix.

The author is also indebted to those who read part or all of the manuscript and who gave many helpful suggestions. He is especially indebted to W. Randolph Burgess, who took the time to read the chapters dealing with the period prior to the mid-thirties; to Merritt Sherman, Secretary, and Lewis N. Dembitz, Division of Research and Statistics, Board of Governors; and to Karl R. Bopp, David P. Eastburn, Evan B. Alderfer, and Lawrence Murdoch of the Federal Reserve Bank of Philadelphia. Even though others have given many valuable suggestions, the author accepts full responsibility for the views expressed. It should be added that these views do not necessarily represent those of this Bank or the Federal Reserve System.

The author owes a special debt of gratitude to Kathryn Kalmbach for assistance with the research and preparation of

---

[1] Minutes of the Federal Open Market Committee from 1936–1960 were recently made available, as mentioned in the Foreword. Minutes of the Open Market Investment Committee for several years in the twenties were made available with the Harrison papers.

the index, and to Charles J. Mustoe for assistance throughout the project, including preparation of the index, editing and preparation of the manuscript for publication. Credit is also due Donald Hulmes for the art work and format.

Last but not least is a special obligation to my wife for assistance with parts of the manuscript, for encouragement throughout my career, and for the tranquility conducive to concentration in the many evenings devoted to this project.

May, 1965   C.J.A.

CONTENTS

PROLOGUE

The more extensive a man's knowledge of what has been done,
the greater will be his power of knowing what to do.

—Disraeli

Money has long been a periodically troublesome problem, not
only for individuals but for nations as well. For centuries, governments had direct control over coinage and the issue of paper
money. History records numerous instances of debasement of
coin, overissue of paper currency, and depreciation in the value
of money. It was so much easier to create more money than to
collect more taxes to meet emergency expenditures that government officials not infrequently succumbed to the temptation.

With the development of private commercial banks, demand
deposits or checking accounts became an important means of
payment. The total volume of bank deposits expanded and con-
tracted as banks responded to increases and decreases in customer demands for credit. Private enterprise, guided by the profit
motive, proved to be an ineffective regulator of the money supply
in the public interest. Creation of too much money sometimes resulted in inflation and depreciation of the currency; too little contributed to financial panics, deflation, and depression. Demonstrated deficiencies of both government and private control of the
money supply was an important reason for a wave of central
banks established in the early part of the present century.

Central banks have a long history. The Bank of Sweden was
established in 1668, the Bank of England in 1694, the Bank of
France in 1800, the Bank of the Netherlands in 1814, and the
Reichsbank in 1875. The First Bank of the United States was
established in 1791, and continued in operation until 1811. The
Second Bank of the United States was chartered in 1816 for a
20-year period. But functions and responsibilities of early institutions differed from those of a modern central bank.

Some central banks were established to help finance the government. Most early central banks had two major functions: banker for the government, and right of note issue. These functions gave the central bank considerable prestige. As it gained prestige and public confidence, commercial banks began holding some of their cash balances in the form of a deposit in the central bank. Thus central banks gradually became custodians of much of the cash reserve of the banking system and the country's gold reserve.

The essence of modern central banking is discretionary control of credit and the money supply. As custodian of the ultimate reserve, central banks began to formulate policy and take actions needed to protect the reserve. The principles enunciated by Walter Bagehot, a noted English economist of the latter half of the 19th century, regarding central bank policy in a period of financial crisis were widely quoted. He said that in a time of crisis the Bank of England should use its reserve and lend freely to avert panic and runs on commercial banks, but lending should be at a high rate to discourage unnecessary borrowing.

Recurring crises revealed a close relation between excessive credit expansion and demands likely to be made on a central bank's reserve. Use of Bank Rate to prevent undue credit expansion and an excessive drain on its reserve became established Bank of England policy in the latter part of the 19th century.

The major industrial and commercial countries adopted the gold standard in the latter half of the 19th century, and protecting the gold reserve became a primary objective of central bank policy. Credit expansion and rising prices usually affected a country's balance of payments adversely and, if long continued, resulted in an outflow of gold. Credit contraction, high interest rates, and falling prices tended to produce an inflow of gold. Gold flows became an important determinant of central bank policy and Bank Rate its chief instrument. An outflow of gold was a signal for an increase in the rate to check credit expansion and a drain on the reserve. Reserve accumulation was a signal that the rate could be reduced.

The role of a central bank prior to World War I was a limited one. Its actions were directed primarily toward avoiding an external drain on the gold reserve, and at times an internal drain arising from excessive credit expansion and speculation.

Development of central banking accelerated following World War I both in terms of the number of central banks and the scope of their responsibilities. A large number of central banks were established following World War I, and today most independent countries have a central bank.

Post-World War I also brought major changes in responsibilities of the central bank. War financing and its aftermath of boom and depression focused attention on internal economic conditions and the need for greater business and price stability. With abandonment of the international gold standard, policymakers had to look for objectives and guides that were suitable in the new environment. Reappraisal of the role of a central bank led to development of more comprehensive objectives, new and more involved techniques designed to achieve them, and much greater emphasis on domestic economic conditions.

There is now considerable uniformity among countries as to the general objectives and functions of a central bank. Its primary responsibility is to regulate credit and the money supply in the public interest. Generally accepted goals are to help maintain reasonably full employment and use of resources, a stable level of prices, sustained economic growth, and to help protect the value of the currency in foreign exchange markets. In addition, the central bank usually serves as banker and fiscal agent of the national government, custodian of cash reserves of the banking system, and a clearing center for collection of checks.

1. LAUNCHED ON THE EVE OF WAR

It should never be lost to sight that the Reserve Banks are invested with much of the quality of a public trust. They were created because of the existence of certain common needs and interests, and they should be administered for the common welfare—for the good of all.

—First Annual Report of the Federal Reserve Board, 1914

The seven members of the first Federal Reserve Board took the oath of office on August 10, 1914, and the 12 Federal Reserve Banks opened for business November 16, 1914. At the end of 1914, the Federal Reserve System had less than 400 employees; today it has nearly 20,000.

Those officials who had the responsibility of organizing this new central banking system in the latter part of 1914 faced a perplexing task. None had any experience in central banking but they recognized that the Federal Reserve System was a unique type of institution which should be operated "for the good of all." The Federal Reserve Act provided a comprehensive legal framework within which the new System was to operate, but offered little guidance as to goals it was expected to achieve.

The outbreak of war in Europe in 1914 disrupted financial relations among the major industrial and commercial countries. Europeans dumped their holdings of American securities, the securities market in New York was demoralized, securities prices dropped sharply, and initially there was a serious drain on the country's gold stock. The first Annual Report of the Federal Reserve Board, describing conditions when the System began operations, stated: "Seldom, if ever, has the banking and business community of the country found itself in a situation of such uncertainty and perplexity."

1

Federal Reserve authorities were confronted with the task of launching a new central bank in an economic environment deranged by a major war. The President of the Federal Reserve Bank of New York, later described the task in these words:

> *In the middle of October, 1914, these 24 men who are responsible for the management of each of the reserve banks, . . . were literally handed the Federal reserve act and told to have these banks open for business on the 16th of November. . . . There wasn't any man living in this country who had had any experience in that kind of banking. . . . Not only that, but it was at a time when the world was in the midst of the greatest war ever fought, and after two and one-half years these infants, so to speak, were called upon to conduct the business in the field of the Treasury of the United States, which in turn had to finance our own war efforts and a very large part of that of the allied countries.*[1]

The new officials faced three major problems: implementing the operating functions provided for in the Act; trying to resolve jurisdictional questions and disputes; and determining the role and policy functions of the new central bank.

Long and frequent were the early meetings of the official groups—the Federal Reserve Board, the Governors of the Federal Reserve Banks, and the Chairmen and Federal Reserve agents of the Federal Reserve Banks.[2] A large part of the discussions was devoted to organizational and operational problems. For instance, items on the agenda for discussion at the second Conference of Presidents of the Reserve Banks in January, 1915, included the cipher code, distribution of organization expenses, commercial paper, revenue warrants, credit information for member banks, settlements between Federal Reserve Banks, use of Reserve Banks as redemption agencies for national bank notes, bonding of employees, recent ruling of the Comptroller of the Currency with respect to national bank notes, definition of time

---

[1] U.S. Congress, *Agricultural Inquiry*, Hearing before the Joint Commission of Agricultural Inquiry, 67th Cong., 1st Sess. (Washington: U.S. Government Printing Office, 1922), Vol. II, pp. 812–813. He was referring to the 12 Governors and 12 Chairmen and Federal Reserve Agents of the Reserve Banks.

[2] Prior to reorganization under the Banking Act of 1935, the Board of Governors was known as the Federal Reserve Board and the titles of Governor and Vice Governor of the Board corresponded to the current titles of Chairman and Vice Chairman. The president of a Reserve Bank then had the title of Governor. To avoid confusion, *the current titles are used throughout the remainder of the study*, except in footnote references to official sources.

deposits, waiver of demand notice and protest, loans to member banks secured by commercial paper, collection of notes by one Reserve Bank for another, acceptances, reports of member banks, clearing-house relations, meaning of lawful money, issue of Federal Reserve notes, borrowed securities, newspaper articles, initiation of changes in rates of discount, and regulations governing commercial paper. There were 76 items on the agenda for the fourth Conference of Presidents in mid-1915 and, according to the Conference Chairman, there were a number of other topics that should be discussed.

Division of authority between the Reserve Banks and the Board of Governors, and between the Federal Reserve agent and president of each Reserve Bank was not clearly defined in the Federal Reserve Act. The result was time-consuming discussion, interpretation, and frequent controversy. For instance, at the second Conference of Presidents of the Reserve Banks in January, 1915, the Chairman thought the authority of the Reserve Banks and the Board of Governors, respectively, in changing the discount rate was so important each president was asked to give his views and those of his board of directors. The consensus was that the board of directors of the Reserve Bank had authority under the law to establish the discount rate. Vesting this authority in the Reserve Bank was considered logical inasmuch as Reserve Bank officials were more familiar with local conditions and therefore what the regional discount rate should be. The Board of Governors had the authority and duty to review the rate established by the Reserve Banks. Several of the presidents stated their boards of directors resented Board interference in making suggestions as to what the discount rate should be.

A similar question brought up for discussion was whether a Reserve Bank desiring to rediscount with another Reserve Bank should apply to the Board of Governors or make its application directly to the Reserve Bank. Some of the presidents thought the application should go to the Board of Governors; others thought it should be made directly to the Reserve Bank subject to approval of the Board.

Another source of frequent controversy was the division of authority between the Federal Reserve agent appointed by the

Board of Governors and the president appointed by the Reserve Bank's board of directors subject to approval by the Board of Governors. A frequent complaint among the presidents was that letters and interpretations of the Board mailed to Federal Reserve agents were either not passed along, or if so only after considerable delay, to the president of the Reserve Bank who had to implement them.

These illustrations suffice to make clear that System officials were initially preoccupied with problems of organization and operations. But there were other factors that tended to divert official thinking away from monetary policy.

Member banks had ample reserves as a result of gold imports and lower reserve requirements for national banks under the Federal Reserve Act. There was little reason for member banks to rediscount at the Reserve Banks. Reserves of the Federal Reserve Banks also were growing, and by the spring of 1917 the combined reserve ratio was around 80 per cent. A shortage of literature on central banking made it more difficult for inexperienced officials to gain a working knowledge of policy issues and problems. Principles developed by the Bank of England were apparently known to several Federal Reserve officials but were not considered appropriate to conditions in the United States.

ROLE OF A CENTRAL BANK

Despite preoccupation with operating problems, officials were concerned as to the appropriate role and functions of the new central bank. Discussions at official meetings revealed several ideas but no consensus as to the System's aims and responsibilities.

On one thing there seemed to be a consensus; the Federal Reserve should be administered for the common welfare—the good of all. It should never permit itself to become the instrument for promotion of the selfish interests of any private or sectional group. Some thought the System should try to be a "steadying influence" at all times, protecting business from the harmful stimulus and consequences of ill-advised credit expansion, and from unnatural credit stringencies and exorbitant interest rates. In order to be in a position to perform this stabilizing influence, resources of the Reserve Banks should be invested in short-term liquid paper which could be readily converted into cash in time of need. Management of the Reserve Banks should strive for better adaptation of the credit mechanism to the needs of industry, commerce, and agriculture. Accommodating commerce and business was soon to become the most important peacetime objective of Federal Reserve policy. Another view expressed was that the Reserve Banks should not be regarded as emergency institutions, their resources kept idle for use only in times of difficulty. They should try to anticipate emergencies and do what they could to prevent them.

PREWAR VIEWS ON POLICY

In the initial years, most of the discussion about policy related to discount rates with occasional reference to other aspects of policy.

Objectives

The only specific statement about policy objectives in the Act was that discount rates should be established, "with a view of accommodating commerce and business; . . . ."

Officials followed a narrow interpretation of accommodating commerce and business. They believed a major aim of policy should be making credit available for "legitimate" business purposes at reasonable rates. This concept of the objective of policy had two significant implications: the volume of Reserve Bank credit should respond to the needs of commerce and business, and it envisaged a passive policy. System officials did not consider it their responsibility to take positive actions to initiate credit and monetary expansion or contraction.

Structure of discount rates

It is not surprising that early discussions of policy dealt mainly with discount rates. Rates at which eligible paper would be discounted for member banks had to be established when the Reserve Banks opened for business. Then, too, the discount rate, or Bank Rate, as it was called in England, had been the primary tool of central bank policy.

Divergent views arose immediately among Federal Reserve officials, not only as to lines of authority in establishing the discount rate but also as to the structure of discount rates and principles that should govern changes in the rate. These differences reflected diffusion of authority among a large number of officials, lack of understanding as to the unique role of a central bank in contrast to commercial banks and other private financial institutions, and absence of well-developed principles governing discount rate policies that appeared appropriate for the United States.

Reflecting largely market practices, the tendency was to establish a structure of discount rates. There was general support for preferential rates on shorter maturities such as 10- to 30-day paper. Lower rates for short maturities conformed to market practices and might also encourage the use of "liquid" paper.

Some officials favored a preferential rate on certain types of eligible paper. A lower rate on bankers acceptances was considered desirable, not only because of their high quality but to encourage development of an acceptance market in the United States. A broader acceptance market, by facilitating financing, would encourage United States exports.

In the fall of 1915, the Board of Governors exerted considerable pressure on the Reserve Banks to establish a preferential rate on paper drawn to finance staple agricultural products, especially cotton.[3] The principal reason given was that a preferential rate would tend to support the price of cotton and other staple commodities, and benefit producers and shippers of agricultural products. One official thought it would be a good public relations move for the new institution.

Most Reserve Bank presidents, however, were strongly opposed to a preferential rate on a certain type of paper. In the first place, preferential rates would be discriminatory, and in effect would give preferred treatment to certain classes of people and types of business. Second, such rates would be difficult to administer. For example, a staple commodity in one region might not be so re-

---

[3] Some officials thought the pressure stemmed mainly from the Secretary of the Treasury (and ex officio Chairman of the Board); they thought he had succumbed to pressure by influential Congressmen from agricultural regions.

garded in another. Third, preferential rates might encourage speculative holding of staple commodities from the market instead of a smooth flow from producer to consumer. Finally, establishing rates to influence prices of certain commodities was not a proper function of the Federal Reserve System.

This initial trend toward preferential discount rates based on maturity and certain classes of paper did not last long. When the United States entered the war, preferential rates were established on Government paper which soon became the primary means of access to Reserve Bank credit. In the postwar period, once the Treasury's financing problems were out of the way, preferential rates were removed except for somewhat lower rates on bankers acceptances to encourage development of an acceptance market.

Discount rate policy

The discount rate structure was soon overshadowed in policy discussions by the more significant question of how to determine an appropriate level of discount rates and when rates should be changed. Principles and guides referred to in early discussions of discount rate policy varied widely. Some were relevant to central bank policy; others were not.

Some officials believed the discount rate should be slightly above market rates for commercial paper to discourage member-bank borrowing for profit. This view reflected the influence of the Bank of England's policy of a penalty rate for the lender of last resort. Federal Reserve officials, however, were aware that different institutional conditions in the United States made it extremely difficult to apply this principle. There was also concern over the attitude of member banks toward discounting. Many member banks looked upon the new Reserve Banks as a source of credit that could be leaned on in time of need; hence they could pursue a more liberal credit policy than formerly. A discount rate that would enable member banks to meet legitimate credit demands of their customers at a reasonable rate but without stimulating excessive or unsound expansion was frequently mentioned.

There were other ideas on the discount rate. One proposal was that it should reflect supply and demand, the rate being raised as the volume of rediscounts at the Reserve Bank increased and vice versa. The Reserve Bank's reserve ratio was also mentioned. There seemed to be a consensus that discount rates should vary among Reserve Districts as needed to meet regional conditions.

Some suggestions reflected complete misunderstanding of the functions of a central bank. One such proposal was that the discount rate should enable the Reserve Bank to keep its resources employed and thus provide earnings. Another was that the discount rate should be somewhat lower than the rate large city banks charged their correspondents.

Open market and foreign operations

The Board of Governors gave the Reserve Banks authority to make purchases in the open market in December, 1914. Some of the Reserve Banks made purchases before the end of the year. Most of the others soon began purchasing certain eligible paper and securities in the open market. Such purchases did not reflect an intention to use open market operations as a tool of monetary policy.

The primary objective of early open market purchases was to acquire additional earnings to help pay expenses. Several Reserve Bank officials said they planned to keep funds not absorbed by rediscounts invested in municipal warrants, bankers acceptances, and Government obligations. Nevertheless, monetary effects of open market operations were recognized as early as 1915. For instance, one Reserve Bank in its annual report to the Board of Governors in 1915, stated it intended to go into the open market, when necessary, to make its rate effective. Another Reserve Bank reported the same year that its influence on interest rates, and credit expansion and contraction was more likely to be exercised through open market operations than member-bank rediscounts because only a small volume of rediscounts was anticipated.

Steps toward centralized purchases were initiated in 1915. New York was the primary market for eligible paper and securities, and it was soon recognized that the Reserve Banks in making purchases independently were often competing against each other. To avoid bidding against each other, some Reserve Banks asked the Federal Reserve Bank of New York to purchase municipal warrants and other eligible paper for them. This was the initial step toward centralized purchases, with the paper and securities being allocated among the Reserve Banks according to an agreed formula.[4] Each Reserve Bank, even though participating in centralized purchases, reserved the right to make purchases independently. Some officials thought a Reserve Bank should act as a dealer in Government securities for member banks in its district, buying from those desiring to sell and selling to those wanting to buy.

Policy toward gold and foreign operations soon came up for discussion. The outbreak of war in Europe and stepped-up purchases in the United States resulted in a substantial inflow of gold. Federal Reserve officials wanted to prevent this gold from serving as the basis for an abnormal expansion of loans so that when gold began to flow out (as they thought it would sooner or later) there would not be a violent contraction of credit with adverse effects on business.

Techniques discussed for mobilizing gold into the Reserve Banks included: paying out Federal Reserve notes for gold, and proposing an amendment to the Federal Reserve Act to permit Federal Reserve notes to be backed 100 per cent by gold. The Board of Governors also recommended an amendment to give the Board authority to raise reserve requirements in emergencies. The purpose was to enable the Board to check any tendencies toward excessive loan expansion in prolonged periods of ease.

Early in 1916, there was considerable discussion of whether the Federal Reserve Banks should plan to engage in foreign operations. The President of the Federal Reserve Bank of New York brought up the question at the Conference of Presidents and discussed it with the Board of Governors. The objective of foreign operations as then visualized was to make investments abroad when profitable, or when desirable for other reasons. It was suggested somewhat later that the reserves of the United States might be better protected if the Federal Reserve had a large fund abroad in foreign bills to draw on in case demands were made for gold.

---

[4] For a while the Federal Reserve Bank of New York was compensated for the expense incurred in making purchases and allocations among participating Reserve Banks.

Some officials thought arrangements might be worked out which would enable the Federal Reserve to influence foreign exchange rates and gold flows. To conduct such operations an agent might be selected and an office provided in the Federal Reserve Bank of New York. He would be under the supervision of the Board of Governors and the President of the Federal Reserve Bank of New York.[5]

UNDERWRITING WAR FINANCING

Federal Reserve officials had little opportunity to crystallize their thinking on the role of Federal Reserve policy before the United States entered the war in the spring of 1917. Soon after the declaration of war, the Secretary of the Treasury transferred important fiscal agency functions to the Reserve Banks. He also asked each Reserve Bank to serve as a central agency in its district for organizing and promoting the sale of Treasury bonds, as well as handling subscriptions, payment, and delivery of the securities.

The new fiscal agency functions resulted in a sharp rise in volume of work handled by the Reserve Banks. Recruiting and training additional staff needed to handle the soaring volume of work absorbed much of the time and thought of System officials. It was a serious limitation on the time that could be devoted to study and development of Federal Reserve policy.

Treasury financing

Treasury officials soon developed the basic principles followed in financing the war. Short-term Treasury certificates of three to six months maturity were issued as funds were needed in anticipation of receipts at tax-payment dates and from periodic flotations of

---

[5] Of historical significance is the fact that successful operation of the gold settlement fund inspired the Board of Governors to propose, in 1918, that an international gold fund be established to avoid shipments of gold from one country to another. The idea was that participating nations would deposit their share of the gold fund in a Government bank so that transfers could be made through the fund without physical transfer of gold, thus avoiding transportation charges, loss from abrasion, and loss of interest while gold was in transit. The Board thought such a fund would be a great advantage to world trade and suggested that initially, participation should be limited to the United States, its Allies, and a few of the leading neutral nations. It was expected that participation might later be extended to practically all countries.

Liberty Bonds. These certificates served two principal purposes. They were an interim source of funds, pending receipts from more permanent forms of financing. It was also expected that these short-term certificates would absorb savings as they accumulated; in effect, enable taxpayers and buyers of Liberty Bonds to distribute payment over the several months interval between tax-payment dates and between flotations of Liberty Bonds.

Treasury officials relied primarily on patriotism, vigorous sales promotion, and a ready availability of credit at low rates to sell the amount of securities needed in helping finance the war. The Secretary of the Treasury vigorously objected to the view that the financing should be done at market rates. Borrowing at market rates would increase the cost of the war and make it difficult for essential industries to obtain credit on reasonable terms.

In order to sell Treasury securities bearing low coupon rates, Treasury officials wanted credit readily available at low rates. Beginning with the first bond flotation, institutions and individuals were urged to borrow, if necessary, in order to buy Government securities. The Secretary of the Treasury wanted Federal Reserve officials to adjust discount rates to the rates on Treasury securities, and wanted those borrowing to buy securities to be able to carry their bank loans at little or no net cost; i.e., the rate on the loan being about the same as the coupon rate on the securities pledged as collateral.

Federal Reserve policy

The newly assigned fiscal functions in which the Federal Reserve served as agent of the Treasury probably had some influence on System thinking as to the role of Federal Reserve policy. War financing was regarded as the responsibility of the Treasury and the Government. For example, the Annual Report of the Federal Reserve Board for 1917 stated: "The Federal Reserve Board is not responsible for the financial policy of the Government, except in so far as the Secretary of the Treasury may choose to call upon its members for service in an advisory capacity." The primary objective of Federal Reserve policy was to facilitate Treasury financing. The Chairman of the Board of Governors stated with reference to System policy and financing the defense effort: "Everything else was thrown into the background. The Board necessarily was obliged to follow the policies of the Treasury Department and the Government." Secondary objectives were to make credit readily available to essential industries, curtail its use for nonessential purposes, and to maintain the financial strength of the Reserve Banks.

Discount rate policy was directed toward making credit readily available for the purchase of Treasury securities. Preferential rates were established on advances to member banks collateralled by Government securities. The preferential rates were kept in line with the coupon rates on Treasury obligations, usually below the coupon rate on current issues. In addition, the Board of Governors authorized the Reserve Banks to discount notes of non-member banks collateralled by Government securities, when endorsed by a member bank, if the proceeds had been or were to be used to purchase Treasury obligations. The Federal Reserve Bank of New York established a 2 to 4 per cent discount rate on one-day advances as a means of restoring to the market, funds temporarily withdrawn by Government operations.[6]

Federal Reserve authorities urged curtailment of credit for nonessential purposes in order to conserve credit as well as goods for production and other activities essential to the war effort. Banks were asked to make credit readily available for Treasury financing and for essential production, but to curtail its use for other purposes.

---

[6] The Board of Governors, at the request of the Secretary of the Treasury, administered foreign exchange regulations and passed on proposed new issues of securities.

In November, 1917, the Secretary, with approval of the President of the United States, designated the Board of Governors as agent of the Secretary in administering foreign exchange regulations. A committee of the Board met daily to consider and pass on applications. The major consideration was whether the proposed transaction was necessary to obtain essential commodities and therefore whether it was in the national interest.

In January, 1918, the Secretary of the Treasury requested the Board to assume the responsibility of passing upon proposed new securities issues and capital expenditures. A subcommittee of the Board was formed to discharge this responsibility and an advisory committee was established consisting of people from the trade. The principal tests applied to proposed new securities issues were whether the offering was timely with respect to Treasury financing operations, and whether the proceeds were to be used in ways that would be in the public interest. In April, 1918, a Capital Issues Committee was created by an Act of Congress and thus superseded the subcommittee of the Board of Governors.

Use of moral suasion to conserve credit for Government financing and essential production reflected a desire to maintain financial strength. It was considered a means of having more credit available for high-priority uses. The policy also reflected a desire to avoid completely unrestrained credit expansion. There appeared to be fairly general recognition among Federal Reserve officials that rapid growth of credit during the war was one cause of rising prices, but opinions differed as to its importance. Some believed the shortage of basic materials and commodities in relation to swollen domestic and foreign demands would have generated a substantial rise in prices even if there were no increase in bank credit.

Support via discount window

Federal Reserve policy made Reserve Bank credit readily available at the discount window at relatively low rates. In addition, member banks were encouraged to borrow from the Reserve Banks to the extent necessary to purchase their quota of Treasury securities and to enable the banks to make loans to their customers for the same purpose. Federal Reserve officials along with commercial bankers urged individuals and business firms to buy their quotas even if they had to borrow a substantial part of the purchase price.

Federal Reserve policy, in effect, provided strong support for the prices of Government securities although not at a rigid pattern as in World War II. Credit was readily available to purchase and to carry the securities at little or no net cost.

2. POST-WORLD WAR I: BOOM AND DEPRESSION

Deflation for the sake of deflation, or of correcting injustices wrought by inflation, is not one of the purposes of the Federal Reserve System.

—John Perrin[1]

Once World War I was over, discussion turned toward an appraisal of the effects and implications of war financing policies. Officials recognized that borrowing to finance the war had resulted in substantial credit expansion, but they did not think Federal Reserve policy had been a significant factor. They stressed that credit expansion was inevitable to the extent that savings fell short of meeting the Government's borrowing needs. Savings did fall short and therefore no reasonable interest rate would have enabled the Government to meet its borrowing needs without credit expansion. Had the Federal Reserve followed the traditional policy of maintaining discount rates above market rates, the Treasury's difficulties would have been increased without any substantial effect on credit expansion.

Neither was credit expansion a major cause of the large wartime demand for goods and services. In their opinion it reflected mainly high wages and soaring profits—not expansion of credit. Under these conditions it was easy for producers to add cost increases to selling prices.

Looking to the future, there was general agreement that transition from war to peace would bring numerous problems and readjustments, including depression and unemployment. Many Government contracts for goods and services would be cancelled; industries producing for war would have to convert to civilian

[1] Chairman and Federal Reserve Agent, Federal Reserve Bank of San Francisco; statement made October, 1920.

production; cutbacks in production accompanying reconversion, and demobilization of returning soldiers would result in substantial unemployment; and readjustments would bring declining prices. There was still a large overhang of undigested Government securities being carried on credit, and a large amount of Treasury financing yet to be done.

In the foreign field, Government loans to foreign countries during the war totaled about $9 billion, and only a limited amount of funds was available for more loans. To retain the existing volume of exports, it might be necessary to extend credit for the purchase of United States goods. Foreigners held large deposits in United States banks and there was concern that once restrictions were removed some balances might be shifted to other countries, resulting in an outflow of gold. German indemnity payments would also be a disturbing factor in international financial operations.

BOOM, NOT DEPRESSION

The end of the war was soon followed by a surge of spending, credit expansion, speculation, and rising prices; not unemployment and depression, as widely expected. Official discussions and reports in 1919 were studded with such terms as extravagant and wasteful spending on luxuries and nonessentials, and an orgy of speculation in securities and commodities. The Board of Governors in its Annual Report stated that 1919 was characterized by:

> . . . an unprecedented orgy of extravagance, a mania for speculation, over-extended business in nearly all lines and in every section of the country, and general demoralization of the agencies of production and distribution. . . . It was universally realized that there would be sooner or later reaction and readjustment, ...[2]

The President of a Federal Reserve Bank stated that a tendency toward speculation began to develop and "by gradual stages it worked up and matured into a veritable orgy of extravagance, waste, and speculation; there was, in fact, a competition to buy

[2] Annual Report of the Federal Reserve Board, 1920, p. 1.

anything at almost any price. This culminated in the early summer of 1920."

As to the credit situation, there was a large overhang of Government securities being carried on credit. Credit was also being used for speculation in securities and for extravagant spending on luxuries and nonessentials. Many member banks were borrowing excessively from the Reserve Banks. One Reserve Bank official said the attitude of member banks was, "to open vigorously the credit throttle, Federal Reserve Banks being relied upon to manipulate the steering wheel. There was apparently a vague idea that brakes were not required." The predominant view among System officials was that the credit problem associated with the postwar boom was primarily one of misuse of credit for such purposes as speculation and extravagant spending for luxuries and nonessentials.

The President of the Federal Reserve Bank of Boston thought the problem was more pervasive. He emphasized that it was not the use of credit for speculation and nonessential activities alone that had contributed to the boom. Credit was being used to bid for materials and to build up inventories in essential as well as nonessential industries. The result was rising prices, still more bidding for materials and inventory, which in turn stimulated making future contracts in anticipation of higher prices. The whole process was cumulative. Speculation, in the sense of action taken in anticipation of higher prices, permeated the entire economy. It was not restricted to securities or certain types of commodities. His views are summarized by the following excerpts from the minutes of November, 1919:

I think the greatest harm is done by the low [discount] rate, because it causes a constant increase in prices. You take our industrial concerns in Boston, and they are urged to take contracts away ahead, continuously further ahead, for their material which they produce. *** Well, what can he do to protect himself? Money is cheap, credit is easy, and he goes ahead, perhaps, and buys his raw material, all he will need for a year, and the contract is effective, and he takes it. He goes into the market to buy his material, and he puts the price up on himself, and when you get all the concerns offered these contracts, because prices are going to be higher in six months or a year, and everybody bidding for that material to protect himself, you get a constantly advancing price, and I believe that the fundamental reason for that is that, whatever else may go up, *credit is cheap and plentiful. The mere fact that it is cheap is evidence that it is plentiful, and I believe that that is what the effect is principally from low rates, and I think that is the greatest harm.* *** *I would not stop at a slightly higher [discount] rate if it was necessary to stop it. I would adopt a policy of high rates. I would like the people to understand that that was the policy of the Federal Reserve Banks, and I should advance those rates until I got control of the situation.*[3]

Policy objectives

Policy formulation was influenced by two main objectives: assisting the Treasury with its difficult postwar financing problems, and dealing with the credit situation.

Federal Reserve officials recognized that the end of the war did not terminate the Treasury's financing problems. In addition to new borrowing, substantial refundings were needed to get the outstanding debt in more manageable form.

The second objective was to get rid of "excessive" borrowing, both by member banks and their customers, without curtailing credit for "legitimate" business. The problem, in the opinion of a majority of the officials, was to prevent extension of credit for speculation and other nonessential purposes, and to bring about liquidation of such credit already outstanding. Referring to speculative uses of credit, one Federal Reserve official stated near the end of 1919: "For the longer this volume of credit remains in use in excess of our requirements for producing and distributing goods and carrying on the usual business of the country, the longer will be delayed a return to more normal business and price conditions."

These objectives called for conflicting actions. Continuation of low rates was desirable in order to facilitate Treasury financing and to avoid inflicting losses on those holding Government securities with borrowed funds. Some form of restraint was needed to prevent credit from feeding the boom. Conflicting objectives and disagreement as to the type of action that should be taken were major influences on System policy during the postwar expansion.

---

[3] Proceedings of a Conference of the Federal Reserve Board with the Governors of the Federal Reserve Banks, November 19–21, 1919, Vol. II, pp. 249–250, 253–254.

Continue the preferential rate?

Early in the postwar period, there was considerable discussion as to how long the preferential rate on advances to member banks collateralled by Government securities should be maintained. There seemed to be general agreement that, with the war over, more consideration should be given to the System's main responsibility of pursuing policies appropriate to the private credit situation. But there was little sentiment for removing the preferential rate on Governments in the near future. One Reserve Bank president, strongly in favor of getting member banks to liquidate their indebtedness as soon as possible to restore a more "normal" credit situation, stated the optimism of some officials reminded him of the fellow who fell out of the 20th story window of a building and as he passed the 10th story said, "I'm all right so far."

Despite an awareness of the unhealthy credit situation and developing boom, the preferential rate was maintained through 1919. Several factors were decisive in the prolonged delay in terminating it. Most important, perhaps, was the resolute resistance of the Secretary of the Treasury. He stressed that removal of the preferential rate or any increase in the discount rate would seriously interfere with Treasury financing. Moreover, an increase in the discount rate would be ineffective; curtailing use of credit for speculative and other nonessential purposes could be better achieved by "direct pressure" in administering discounts and advances. Not until early 1920 did Treasury officials think debt management problems were well enough in hand for discount rate policy to be directed toward other objectives.

Another important reason for delay in removing the preferential rate or in raising the discount rate on commercial paper was a strong conviction among Federal Reserve officials that they had a moral obligation not to "pull the rug out" from under those who had responded to official urging to borrow and buy Government securities. There was also fear that an increase in discount rates would result in widespread liquidation of Government securities and possibly drastic declines in securities prices.

As the Treasury's financing problems became less pressing and as the business boom accelerated, sentiment in favor of terminating the preferential rate increased. At the Presidents' Conference in April, 1920, only three of the 12 presidents favored discontinuance. But as time passed there was growing recognition that the preferential rate was the effective rate because member banks pledged collateral that was entitled to the lower rate. By the fall of 1920, the presidents agreed that a uniform discount rate for all classes of paper should be established in the near future.

Direct pressure

Divergent views as to the role of credit and problems of implementation led to sharp disagreement as to how "excessive" credit expansion could best be curtailed.

Those who visualized the credit problem primarily as misuse rather than too much, logically favored a selective approach—attempting to prevent extension of credit for speculative and nonessential uses. They advocated direct pressure, the Reserve Banks refusing to make discounts and advances to member banks for other than legitimate and productive purposes. One System official expressed the opinion that while quantitative controls are useful, intelligent and discriminating policy that withholds credit when it is to be used for nonproductive purposes but does not withhold it to feed production is far better.

Another main argument for direct pressure was that an increase in the discount rate would not be effective. In the fall of 1919, the Secretary of the Treasury in a letter to the Chairman of the Board of Governors urged that the Board take charge of policy and insist that the Reserve Banks exercise firm discrimination in making advances, in order to prevent abuses of Reserve Bank credit facilities instead of relying too much on higher rates. He said the speculative mania in securities, land, and commodities had developed to such an extent that the credit structure was gravely threatened.

The Secretary gave several reasons why the discount rate would not be effective under existing conditions. First, a higher rate would fall lightly on the borrower for speculative purposes because he operates in anticipation of a large profit. Second, a materially higher discount rate might penalize and discourage the commercial and industrial borrower, curtail production, increase the shortage of goods, and thus increase commodity prices. Rising prices would stimulate, not retard, speculation.

Third, an increase in the discount rate would have a "grave effect" upon the Government's finances. Moreover, when the Government's debt was small and owned by permanent holders, possession of eligible paper was strong presumptive evidence of a member bank's right to borrow; however, this was no longer true with a large postwar debt which was widely held. Finally, with the international gold standard having been abandoned, the discount rate would operate solely on the domestic situation. A higher rate would not curb imports or stimulate exports; hence it would have no significant effect on gold flows.

Case for the discount rate

One of the principal arguments for using the discount rate to curb expansion was a practical one; it was impossible to control use of credit by direct pressure through administration of the discount window. Member banks borrow to replenish reserves, and reserve positions are impaired by a variety of transactions including loans already made. Use of the proceeds has usually been determined before the bank asks for an advance. Moreover, even if initial use could be regulated, secondary uses could not. Reserves created by advances to a bank with no speculative loans might well be transmitted via the money market to banks with speculative loans. Neither is it possible to distinguish between essential and nonessential uses of credit, an important reason being that the type of paper offered to the Reserve Bank is no indication of the use to be made of the proceeds.

There were other practical disadvantages of direct pressure via the discount window. Refusing advances to member banks that had already entered into commitments might cause serious difficulty, even failure, whereas an increase in rate would discourage future commitments. Direct pressure would reach only those member banks that were already overextended and borrowing from the Reserve Banks. Competition would seriously impair the effectiveness of direct pressure because of fear that refusing to make loans for certain purposes might result in customers going to another bank which would make the loans.

Those favoring use of the discount rate contended an increase would restrict speculative and nonessential uses of credit. One

Reserve Bank president who thought much of the problem was use of credit for extravagant and wasteful spending favored the discount rate. He thought direct pressure was impossible to implement, but he also believed an increase in the discount rate would effectively curb use of credit for speculation. He stated the first response of New York money-market banks to pressure on their reserve position was to call some of their loans to brokers and dealers.

The most logical argument for use of the discount rate instead of direct pressure was the minority view that low rates were the real source of the credit problem. Cheap and liberal credit encourage anticipatory buying, advance commitments bid up prices, and rising prices stimulate demand for and a further expansion of credit. An increase in the discount rate would be interpreted as a signal that credit was likely to be less plentiful as well as more expensive; as a result, business firms would be discouraged from making advance commitments and building up inventories. Significantly, this argument for rate action stressed availability as well as cost of credit.

HOW TO DEAL WITH EXCESSIVE MEMBER BANK BORROWING?

Substantial support within the System for direct pressure and strong opposition to a rate increase led to a search for methods of curtailing the boom without a general increase in discount rates. The Board of Governors, in a letter of July 10, 1918, to the presidents of the Reserve Banks, had stated the Board was in agreement with the consensus expressed at the Presidents' Conference that excessive rediscounts could be controlled by such techniques as requiring additional collateral and informing member banks they had reached their limit. The Board preferred these methods to a change in discount rates. In fact, the Board had refused the recommendation of one Reserve Bank to advance its discount rate as a means of controlling excessive borrowing.

Additional collateral

Some Reserve Banks required more than 100 per cent collateral for certain advances to member banks. Sometimes the purpose was safety. For example, one Reserve Bank required a margin of at least 20 per cent on advances collateralled by cotton because of the situation in the cotton industry.

But some Reserve Banks used additional collateral as a means of discouraging excessive member-bank borrowing. The larger the amount of borrowing the higher the margin of additional collateral required. At times a number of member banks were putting up as much as 100 per cent additional collateral. In extreme cases of excessive borrowing, additional collateral was sometimes required in order to reduce the amount of paper the banks had available for discount.

Moral suasion

Reserve Bank officials also asked member banks to use discretion in extending credit. One Reserve Bank sent a circular to all of its member banks requesting them not to make speculative loans, including loans to hold commodities for higher prices. Several Reserve Bank officials thought moral suasion had good effects in their districts, but the majority believed moral suasion alone was not sufficient.

Some Reserve Bank officials held conferences with excessive borrowers and used examiners' reports to see whether the banks were making loans for speculation or similar purposes. If found to be making improper use of Reserve Bank credit, the banks were asked to liquidate some of these loans instead of borrowing from the Reserve Bank.

In the spring of 1920, the Board of Governors asked the Reserve Banks to submit a written report of methods employed to keep informed on how member banks were using Reserve Bank credit. Even though the Reserve Banks tried to keep up with the loan and investment policies of their member banks, the presidents were unanimous that it was not practical in peacetime to try to distinguish between essential and nonessential uses of Reserve Bank credit.

Progressive discount rates

The Board of Governors suggested as early as 1918 that Reserve Banks establish a normal line of credit for each member bank and apply graduated discount rates to borrowing in excess of that line. After considering the disadvantages of graduated rates, they decided it would be preferable for Reserve Banks to use moral suasion with member banks borrowing apparently excessive amounts. But in its Annual Report for 1919, the Board recommended to Congress an amendment to the Federal Reserve Act giving authority to establish graduated discount rates. The authority was granted in April, 1920.

Four Reserve Banks—St. Louis, Kansas City, Dallas, and Atlanta—established progressive rates effective in April and May, 1920. The usual surcharge on amounts borrowed in excess of the basic line ranged from ½ per cent to 2½ per cent above the regular discount rate. Unusually high surcharges were paid in only a few cases, and only on small amounts; however, critics sometimes cited without qualification extremely high discount rates paid by some member banks.

The presidents of the Reserve Banks agreed that the basic line should reflect a member bank's fair share of total borrowing from the Reserve Bank. A member's fair share, according to the presidents, should represent its contribution to the lending power of the Reserve Bank, namely the sum of its required reserve plus capital paid into the Reserve Bank. It was agreed, however, that each Reserve Bank should determine the basic line for its member banks; that the method need not be absolutely uniform in all districts. The Reserve Banks which established progressive rates exempted loans against Government securities from computation of the basic line, and some exempted loans against agricultural paper.

Official discussions revealed significant differences of opinion within the System as to the desirability of progressive discount rates. One of the principal arguments for progressive rates was that moral suasion and careful administration of the discount window were not fully effective because member-bank officials always insisted they were borrowing for legitimate purposes. In the words of one of the Reserve Bank presidents, "no words are as persuasive as one and one half per cent." Another advantage was that the cost was increased only on excess borrowings of member banks. Progressive rates enabled a Reserve Bank to maintain a low basic discount rate which would be helpful to business and agriculture.

Some Federal Reserve officials were strongly opposed to progressive rates. A significant weakness for those favoring a selective approach was that it did not discriminate between productive and nonessential uses of credit. Some Reserve Bank presidents thought a progressive rate had less influence on member-bank borrowing than the possibility that a Reserve Bank might refuse to lend. In addition, establishing a basic line might serve as an invitation for member banks to borrow up to that amount. Exempting from the basic line, advances against Government securities and in some cases agricultural paper seriously reduced the effectiveness of progressive rates. Some member banks avoided the surcharge by borrowing from correspondents in Reserve Districts which did not have progressive rates.

A serious inherent weakness of progressive rates apparently received little attention. The basic line provided no evidence that borrowing up to that amount would be for appropriate purposes. Neither was borrowing in excess of the line any indication of inappropriate borrowing. The penalty was automatically applied on the basis of quantity without regard to the reasons for borrowing. Rule was substituted for discretion in administering the discount window. It is not surprising that the four Reserve Banks abandoned their progressive rates within a few months.[4]

---

[4] Two additional proposals for imposing restraint may be of interest to historians even though they did not receive serious consideration. A member of the Board of Governors suggested establishing a ceiling on Federal Reserve note issues. When the ceiling was reached, a Reserve Bank could get additional Federal Reserve notes only by convincing the Board that more notes would contribute to production and would be in the public interest. He thought controlling the note issue was the chief function of the Board and alleged that the ceiling on note issue would stiffen the will power of officials, enable the Reserve Banks to deal more effectively with member banks, and thus provide a more effective method of controlling expansion.

The proposal had little support among other Federal Reserve officials. They believed credit could be regulated more effectively by using the discount rate and discount policy as needed. One member of the Board stated the opposition well in saying that a ceiling on note issue would be like a doctor saying to his patient, "Stop shivering with the ague; from now on you are entitled to only one shiver a day."

In 1920, a proposal was made that the Board of Governors levy a tax on the portion of Federal Reserve note issues not covered by gold (under Section 16 of the Act) to help restrain expansion. The intention was that Reserve Banks with large reserve ratios would pay out gold and gold certificates instead of paying a tax on Federal Reserve notes. The resulting decline in reserve ratios would make a restrictive policy more acceptable to the public.

A NEW PROBLEM: DEPRESSION

Treasury officials informed the Federal Reserve that early in 1920 debt management operations would no longer require that discount rate policy be directed toward facilitating Treasury financing. The fact that the gold reserve ratio of the Federal Reserve Banks was approaching the legal minimum was believed to be another reason for Treasury acquiescence to a more restrictive discount rate policy. The discount rate was increased sharply, the final increase to 7 per cent by some Reserve Banks being made before midyear. The postwar boom reached its peak before mid-1920 and was followed by depression and falling prices.

Federal Reserve officials, who had been striving to find some way to curtail the boom without making credit scarcer and more expensive for Government and for business, were confronted with a new problem. The key to understanding Federal Reserve policy in the depression is the views of System officials as to the causes of business fluctuations.

Why depression?

Federal Reserve authorities were aware of well-defined cycles in business activity. The Annual Report of the Board of Governors for 1921 described cycles in business: rising business activity and increasing production; excessive expansion and speculation followed by panic and forced liquidation; a long period of slow liquidation, business depression, and stagnation; and revival. A member of the Board stated early in 1919: "The most serious part of inflation is, after all, the aftermath. We sow the wind to reap the whirlwind. Somehow or other we have got to come down off the perch." The president of a Reserve Bank stated with reference to the deflation and depression of 1920-1921, "Nature brought it on." The consensus of System officials was that deflation and declining prices were the aftermath of war and were inevitable; that no institution or individual could have prevented either the boom and rising prices or the subsequent decline.

History demonstrated not only that depression always follows war and inflation, but the more intense the boom the more severe the reaction. The Annual Report of the Board for 1921 stated:

. . . if the flow of the incoming tide can be controlled so that the crest may not be reached too rapidly nor rise too high the subsequent reaction will be less severe and the next period of industrial and commercial activity and general prosperity will be marked by saner methods, greater achievement along constructive lines, and by a longer duration than any which we have had before.[5]

Thus the intensity of the postwar boom meant that readjustment and deflation would be more severe.

The above theory of the business cycle was in good standing. There was a general belief that the real injury was done during the period of credit expansion, not during credit contraction which was considered curative. Professor Sprague of Harvard University, one of the most highly esteemed economists of the time, stated with reference to the depression of 1921: "A period of readjustment and liquidation was inevitable. Liberal credits at low rates in 1920 would have deferred its advent somewhat, but with the certain consequence that the difficulty and losses incident to readjustment would have been materially enhanced."[6]

Policy objectives

The depression of 1920–1921 was the first opportunity for Federal Reserve authorities to formulate policy relating to domestic conditions solely on the basis of their own beliefs. During the war and the postwar period until early 1920, policy had been directed toward facilitating Treasury financing. The postwar boom had just about reached its peak when Treasury officials agreed that policy need no longer be directed mainly toward Treasury debt management operations.

What goals shaped System policy during the depression? Were actions directed toward forced liquidation and deflation as sometimes charged?

The answer is a definite no, according to the official record of policy discussions and other statements of officials just prior to and during the depression. The quotation at the beginning of this chapter is a statement made in a joint conference of the three policymaking groups: Board of Governors, presidents of the Reserve Banks, and Federal Reserve agents of the Reserve Banks—

---

[5] Page 99.
[6] *Agricultural Inquiry*, Hearing, *op. cit.*, Vol. II, p. 468.

in the fall of 1920. The Annual Report of the Federal Reserve Board for 1919 stated that credit expansion must be checked but that deflation "merely for the sake of deflation and a speedy return to 'normal'—deflation merely for the sake of restoring securities values and commodity prices to their prewar levels without regard to other consequences, would be an insensate proceeding in the existing posture of national and world affairs."[7]

The primary objective of System policy followed logically from the theory officials had as to the nature and causes of business fluctuations. It was necessary to get rid of the excesses built up during the boom and to restore credit to its "proper" role of financing production and the orderly distribution of goods to consumers. To achieve this objective required orderly liquidation of the excesses and preventing extension of new credit for speculative and nonessential purposes.

"Orderly liquidation," a term frequently used by System officials in this period, referred to readjustments regarded as essential for recovery, proceeding neither too slowly nor too rapidly. If liquidation is too slow, distress and agony are unduly prolonged. If rapid and too drastic, liquidation might precipitate the dumping of topheavy inventories on the market, disorderly decline, and excessive hardship and losses.

A second and closely related problem of implementation was to limit new extension of credit to productive uses. The intention was not necessarily over-all credit contraction; it was an orderly liquidation of credit for speculation, for holding excessive inventories, and other nonessential purposes. New credit should be extended only for productive purposes, and the total increase should not exceed the rise in total volume of production.

These two methods of trying to achieve the primary goal, officials were careful to point out, did not mean they were striving for deflation *per se* or to roll back prices to some former level. They were in agreement that regulating the level of prices was not one of the functions of the Federal Reserve System. But orderly liquidation would tend to moderate the price decline, and restoring sound credit conditions would result in a "healthy price level."

---

[7] Page 72.

Discount policy

Administration of the discount window was an important method of encouraging orderly liquidation. Discussion of this phase of policy lends strong support to the view that officials were seeking orderly but not forced liquidation.

At a joint meeting of the Board of Governors and presidents of the Reserve Banks in April, 1921, there was not a single spokesman in favor of direct pressure to *force* liquidation of loans. The consensus was that any attempt to compel liquidation would bring a further decline of prices, depreciation of the value of collateral, and thus undermine outstanding loans. It was better to try to carry borrowers until market conditions improved and their loans could be repaid. A member of the Board, who was an ardent advocate of the real-bills doctrine, stated that at times like this "direct action, unless applied . . . with utmost discrimination and the fullest knowledge, . . . is little short of destructive and almost criminal." He said the time for direct action was to prevent development of a bad situation, not to correct it. A Reserve Bank president stated in the spring of 1921, "we think it little short of a crime to force the liquidation of commercial commodities at this time, . . ."

A go-around at this April, 1921, meeting revealed that some Reserve Banks had been working with excessive borrowers in an effort to get their indebtedness down to a more reasonable basis; but none had asked the banks to force their customers to liquidate. Reports indicated that member banks sometimes used the Reserve Banks as a crutch to put pressure on large and persistent borrowers to pay up. In fact, a few presidents said member-bank officials had asked them for statements they could use with their large borrowers, but the requests were refused. The fact that member banks were using the Reserve Banks to get some of their large and persistent borrowers to pay up was believed responsible for much of the public criticism that the Federal Reserve was forcing liquidation.

Discount rate policy

Discount rate policy was also directed toward restoring a normal situation in which use of credit would be confined to production and orderly marketing of goods and services. In the spring of 1921, at joint conferences of the Board of Governors with the presidents and a Class B director from each Reserve Bank, there was extended discussion of discount rate policy and whether rates should be lowered. A large majority opposed a reduction at the time. Liquidation was not yet complete. Reduction of discount rates would have little effect on the volume of borrowing from Reserve Banks and might be interpreted as a signal of "loosening up." A number of officials expressed fear that lower rates would only stimulate use of credit for speculation and other ill-advised purposes rather than for legitimate business. Lower rates might also delay needed liquidation and readjustments. Many country banks were over-loaned to help customers carry agricultural products which they did not want to sell at sharply declining prices. The consensus was that the Reserve Banks should work with these banks to help them get out of a difficult situation.

A small minority favored lowering the discount rate. They thought liquidation was mostly complete and a lower rate might encourage expansion.

The theory that depression was a period of liquidation and readjustment essential for a sound business recovery led to a passive rather than a positive Federal Reserve policy. Maintaining discount rates at a high level was considered desirable, both to encourage liquidation of credit excesses built up during the preceding boom and to discourage the use of new credit for nonessential purposes. Bagehot was often quoted in support of a policy of making credit readily available but expensive. There was no sentiment for low discount rates to stimulate recovery. A sound recovery could occur only after essential readjustments had been completed. The Chairman of the Board of Governors, in the spring of 1921, said the Federal Reserve System did not intend to try to correct the existing situation by encouraging a new credit expansion, new inflation, or by the adoption of some nostrum or artificial remedy.

Other policy thoughts

Apprehension in 1921 that gold imports and a rise in the reserve ratio of the Reserve Banks might result in pressure for a reduction in discount rates led to suggestions for offsetting the effect on reserves. One proposal was for Reserve Banks to pay gold coins and gold certificates into circulation. Most Reserve Bank presidents were opposed. They thought gold coins and gold certificates paid out would come right back. Moreover, they were opposed to this method of trying to justify a certain discount rate policy.

Another suggestion was to leave some gold in the Bank of England under earmark where it would not count as reserve of the Reserve Banks. This proposal also gained little support.

In the fall of 1921, there was considerable discussion of the disorganized state of foreign exchange markets. The President of the Federal Reserve Bank of New York thought some method of stabilizing foreign exchange rates had to be worked out as a prerequisite to any real revival of world trade, and that responsibility for doing something rested primarily on the Federal Reserve System. In his opinion, disorderly foreign exchange markets reflected mainly currency inflation in many countries; government budget deficits; imposition of reparation payments on Germany; and possible insistence that foreign governments make their payments of interest and principal to the United States at a faster rate than ordinary processes of trade would permit. He thought several foreign countries—Switzerland, Holland, Denmark, Sweden, Norway, Japan, and England—had their finances in a condition so that it might be possible to stabilize their exchange rates.

In his opinion, one of the best approaches might be establishment of a fund to trade in foreign exchange. The central banks of some of the major countries might join with the United States in establishing a fund—perhaps of about $300 million. A relatively small amount of buying or selling appropriately timed could have a substantial influence on exchange rates. Hence operations in small volume would probably suffice to stabilize exchange rates for countries with balanced budgets and stable currencies.

3. PIONEERING IN POLICY: OBJECTIVES AND GUIDES

The gold standard went in abeyance in 1914. . . . The Reserve system really had nothing, therefore . . . to guide it when it had to face the first serious test after the war. . . . [It] was a good deal like a ship at sea without . . . rudder and compass to guide it. All the old paraphernalia had become . . . useless, and nothing new had been devised. . . . I think it is to the everlasting credit of our Federal reserve system that it soon recognized the need for new instruments of regulation and began to set about their construction.

—Adolph C. Miller, 1926[1]

The next few years, following the depression of 1920–1921, was an era of pioneering in central banking thought. There were three main reasons for the unusual progress during this period.

The war and its aftermath had swept away the environment in which central banking thought had developed. Prewar objectives and guides had been built around the international gold standard. They were oriented toward the balance of payments, foreign exchange rates, and protecting the gold reserve. The gold standard had been abandoned and System officials recognized that the old objectives and principles were not appropriate in the new environment. It was their task to try to develop objectives and policies that would be appropriate.

A second reason was that Federal Reserve officials were relatively free from pressing problems for the first time since the beginning of the System. From 1914 to 1921, they had been preoccupied with a series of problems: organizational, jurisdictional, and operational issues involved in launching the new System in an environment disrupted by war; assisting the Treasury in its

[1] Member of the Board of Governors.

31

war and postwar financing operations; development of the postwar inflationary boom; and finally the severe postwar depression,
widely regarded among System officials as the inevitable aftermath of war and the ensuing boom. Now they were in a position
to concentrate on the policy role and responsibilities of a central
bank. An important step in this direction was the annual conferences of the three policymaking groups: Board of Governors,
presidents of the Reserve Banks, and Federal Reserve agents of
the Reserve Banks—which were devoted primarily to papers and
discussion on various aspects of Federal Reserve policy.

Third, the postwar boom and depression, especially the latter,
were sobering experiences for policymakers. They did not think
credit policy was to blame, but the public was not so generous in
its appraisal. There was widespread criticism of the Federal Reserve. Several Federal Reserve officials were grilled at length in
a Congressional inquiry in 1921, and many influential members
of Congress thought Federal Reserve policy was largely responsible for the depression. This criticism left a deep impression on
System officials and undoubtedly was a strong motive for exploring much more thoroughly just what the Federal Reserve could
and should do.

One of the first tasks was to reappraise the role of the Federal
Reserve. What should it try to achieve? What tests could be used
to determine timing of actions needed to achieve objectives?

POLICY OBJECTIVES

Perhaps for the first time, central bank policy was oriented toward
domestic economic conditions instead of the balance of payments
and the gold reserve.

Accommodating business

From the beginning of the System, accommodating commerce
and business usually entered into policy discussions. Officials considered accommodating business at reasonable rates to be one of
the functions of the Federal Reserve Banks. Following World War I,
accommodating business began to acquire a special meaning
among System officials; it also became a more important objec-

tive. In the spring of 1923, the Board of Governors stated that accommodation of commerce and business should be the principal objective of open market operations.

System officials gave considerable thought to developing tests or standards that could be used to determine when business was being accommodated in a satisfactory manner. The result was development of a particular philosophy as to the role of credit.[2]

The primary function of credit was to help finance production and the orderly distribution of goods from producer to consumer. It was appropriate, therefore, that credit be extended for production, storage and marketing of goods and services. Accommodating business also included meeting seasonal and other temporary needs for credit and currency, and it soon became established Federal Reserve policy to facilitate adjustments to short-term stresses and strain such as arise at quarterly tax-payment dates and during the crop-marketing season.

But officials were careful to point out that certain uses of credit were not consistent with their concept of accommodating commerce and business. Credit should not be used for speculative purposes. According to the Board's Annual Report for 1923, "the economic use of credit is to facilitate the production and orderly marketing of goods and not to finance the speculative holding of excessive stocks of materials and merchandise." Speculative purposes embraced use of credit to hold goods, real estate, or securities in anticipation of higher prices.

A second use inconsistent with the concept of accommodating business was extending credit that results only in higher prices instead of more production. As stated in the Annual Report: "When production reaches the limits imposed by the available supplies of labor, plant capacity, and transportation facilities— in fact, whenever the productive energies and resources of the country are employed at full capacity—output can not be enlarged by an increased use of credit and by further increases in prices." An increase in credit was not justified if it only resulted in one business being able to produce more and another produce less.

---

[2] A good analysis was given in the Annual Report of the Federal Reserve Board, 1923, pp. 29–39.

A corollary of the objective of providing credit only for production and the orderly distribution of goods was prevention of inflation and deflation. Depression was visualized as the inevitable result of an inflationary boom; and booms were generated by improper uses and excessive expansion of credit. Consequently, confining credit to productive uses, as defined above, would automatically prevent inflation and depression; however, should depression occur, this theory called for a passive Federal Reserve policy aimed at facilitating orderly liquidation and readjustment. Aggressive ease to stimulate recovery was considered undesirable.

But as the effects of Federal Reserve actions, especially open market operations, became more fully understood the attitude regarding a passive policy during a slump began to be modified. Open market operations could be used at the Federal Reserve's own initiative to put additional funds in the market. By the mid-1920's, some officials believed an easy money policy should be used in depression to promote recovery, just as restraint should be used to curb a boom.

Price stability

Postwar boom and deflation focused attention on economic hardships imposed by price fluctuations. The relation between the volume of credit and prices was a topic of not infrequent discussion, and proposals were made outside the System that price stability should be a major objective of Federal Reserve policy. In 1926, a bill was introduced in Congress to make stabilization of the price level a statutory objective.

Federal Reserve officials, in extended internal discussions and in testimony at Congressional hearings, expressed vigorous opposition to price stability as a declared objective. They agreed that credit had some influence on prices and that price movements were a factor to be considered in formulation of policy. But they were practically unanimous in their opposition to making price stability a statutory objective.

The core of their opposition derived from a belief that price stability was the result, not the cause of economic stability. According to their theory of business fluctuations, Federal Reserve policy would make its best contribution toward price stability when directed toward maintaining sound credit conditions as described above. |

|Federal Reserve officials had several more specific objections. They believed the price level was determined largely by nonmonetary factors over which they had no control. Therefore, to make the Federal Reserve responsible for price stability would mean the System was doomed to failure in achieving a statutory objective. Second, establishing price stability as a declared objective would be certain to lead to misunderstanding and unjust criticism of the Federal Reserve.\Remembering 1921, officials were fearful that farmers and other producers would expect the Federal Reserve to keep prices of their products stable, and in the event of a decline the System would be held responsible.|Furthermore, the fact that the System could not achieve the established objective would in itself result in criticism. Third, changes in the price level register an accomplished fact. Credit policy should take into consideration factors that work before a change in the price level occurs. The need is for timely action which often should be taken before the chain of events is reflected in the price level. Finally, some officials emphasized that no statistical mechanism or formula is an adequate goal of credit policy.|One Reserve Bank official said: "I do not think that the discount policies of the reserve bank should be determined by watching a chart or an index of the price level." There were too many elusive factors that should be considered to fit them into any mechanical formula.

GUIDES TO POLICY

Goals to be aimed at was only the first step in policy considerations. Papers were given and extended discussion was devoted to guides or tests that would indicate actions needed to achieve objectives. The problem was twofold: conceptual and analytical in the sense of determining what would be effective guides in our economic and financial environment; and development of information needed in order that the guides might be used.

Rules not feasible

Federal Reserve officials seemed to be in complete agreement that effective policy could not be formulated according to some simple rule or mechanical formula. In the early twenties, some economists proposed that rules should be worked out for changing the discount rate so that the public could know what to expect. There was a consensus among Federal Reserve officials that automatic adjustment of the discount rate according to rule or formula was not feasible. One official pointed to experience as demonstrating that developing skill in weighting different factors and varying the weights as conditions change is the most important element in policy formulation. Judgment, not rules, is essential in evaluating the various factors and determining which are the more significant under changing circumstances. Even though objectives remain the same, actions to achieve them will vary according to changes in business and credit conditions.

Use or quality of credit

Use of credit was an important guide referred to in policy discussions but somewhat less important as an actual determinant of actions taken because quantitative tools could not be used to regulate specific uses. If misuse is regarded as a major cause of trouble, then use being made of credit is naturally an important guide as to whether some kind of action is called for.

Some Federal Reserve officials believed that the primary responsibility of a central bank was to maintain sound credit conditions. An important test, the primary one for some officials, was whether credit was being used for speculation in inventories, securities, or real estate. If quality of credit could be preserved, quantity would take care of itself. For example, a member of the Board of Governors stated: "To me the most simple formula of operating the Federal reserve system to give the country stability . . . is to stop and absolutely foreclose the diversion of any Federal reserve credit to speculative purposes."

Few Federal Reserve officials disagreed with the above concept of sound uses of credit. A large number, however, recognized serious practical difficulties in trying to implement such a policy. As explained earlier, the quality or character of the paper offered at the discount window was no indication of the use to be made of the reserves so obtained. Some officials went further, stating that maintaining the quality of paper would not necessarily prevent excessive expansion of credit. One Reserve Bank official pointed out as early as 1922 that the quality of paper offered is essentially the same in extreme inflation as in deflation. The total volume of credit could double with little change in either the volume of physical production or in the quality of the paper. Hence a better test or guide than mere quality was needed.

Other guides

In groping for guides that would be helpful in formulating policy to achieve domestic objectives, System officials were pioneering. It was only natural that discussion ranged over a number of guides.

Prices, although rejected as an objective, were considered a useful guide in policy formulation. But some officials cautioned that price trends should be used with care. In our type of economy there is a general tendency for prices to rise somewhat in a period of business recovery; the rise reflects improved demand. An increase in price is the signal for more production of a commodity. A rise in prices in itself, therefore, is not an adequate test for credit restraint. As long as production is increasing and responding to the price signal, the situation is not too disturbing. The danger point comes when prices are rising but physical output is not. Making more Reserve Bank credit available under these circumstances is both making possible and supporting the price rise.

Uses of credit, relation of credit expansion to volume of production, and price trends were some of the fundamental intermediate-term guides. But more immediate guides were also discussed. Market rates of interest had long been discussed in connection with discount rate policy. A penalty rate was accepted in principle but was recognized as impractical because rates differed too widely, both as to type of paper and regionally. Nevertheless, market rates were usually considered in determining whether a change in the discount rate was desirable. One consideration was a relationship to market rates that would enable member banks to borrow at reasonable rates to meet legitimate business demands, but a rate that would discourage borrowing for purely speculative purposes. Officials of the Federal

Reserve Bank of New York thought that normally a good relationship was to have the New York discount rate between the market rate for commercial paper and the rate for bankers acceptances. The relation between market rates in New York and leading foreign financial centers such as London became a significant factor in the twenties. In order to assist other countries to stabilize their foreign exchange rates and return to the gold standard, officials tried to avoid establishing a discount rate that would attract foreign funds and complicate the stabilization efforts of foreign countries; however, the minutes clearly reveal that assisting foreign countries was secondary to domestic economic conditions in policy formulation.

The volume of borrowing at Reserve Banks was another guide both for discount rate and open market policies. Experience indicated that when member-bank borrowing in the principal financial centers rose substantially, market rates tended to rise above the discount rate and there was real pressure for reducing loans. When borrowing dropped to a very low level, market rates declined below the discount rate and there was a tendency toward credit inflation. A view prevalent among officials, including the Board's director of research, was that abundant credit at low rates—especially if for a prolonged period—would likely lead to marginal uses and a deterioration in the quality of credit. In the mid-twenties, about $50 million was regarded as a comfortable level of borrowing at the Federal Reserve Bank of New York because at that level there was neither marked pressure for liquidation nor too much ease.

The reserve ratio of the Reserve Banks, although frequently mentioned, was not an important determinant of policy during the twenties. An interesting proposal was made early in the decade by a member of the Board of Governors to separate the reserve against Federal Reserve notes from that against Reserve Bank deposits. Gold imports and exports would be reflected in the reserve against notes, making the reserve ratio against deposits a more sensitive indicator of internal expansion and contraction of credit. Most of the Reserve Bank presidents, although sympathetic to having the reserve ratio a more sensitive indicator of business and credit conditions, opposed adoption of the proposal. They were afraid public reaction might be that this was "juggling the reserve figures" with the result that confidence in the Reserve Banks would be impaired.

RESEARCH AND STATISTICS

Federal Reserve officials recognized that in addition to certain short- and intermediate-term guides a large amount of background information was needed. Sufficient data to diagnose the state of the economy were a prerequisite for formulating policy directed toward domestic economic goals.

In the early postwar period, plans were made to develop a series of indices that would reflect changes in business activity, production, trade, employment, prices, and other significant business and financial activities. Suggestions and advice were solicited from such well-known economists as professors Irving Fisher of Yale, Allyn Young of Harvard, and Wesley C. Mitchell of Columbia in developing the statistical program. Walter Stewart, who became director of the Board's Division of Research and Statistics in 1922, made a major contribution in the development and expansion of research activities. The Board also urged the Reserve Banks to expand their statistical work. In order to help coordinate and promote a System-wide program, occasional conferences were held which included representatives of the research staffs of the Board and the Banks. Members of the Board's research staff visited the Reserve Banks to become more familiar with their research and statistical work, and in the mid-1920's a member of the Board's research staff was given the special assignment of keeping informed on research activities in the Reserve Banks.

The primary purpose in expanding the research program was to provide information needed for wise policy decisions. A member of the Board stated that by 1923 the System had developed enough information and had gained enough experience so that the Board had sufficient confidence to explain the working principles of policy formulation in the Annual Report for 1923.

By the mid-twenties a substantial amount of information was being presented at meetings devoted to policy formulation. The

Board's acting director of research and statistics stated: "The central aim in working upon these problems is to obtain results that can be used by the Federal Reserve Board and by the officers of the Federal reserve banks as a part of the basis for policy decisions." Reports on business and financial developments submitted at meetings of the Open Market Investment Committee, for example, included such topics as credit developments, loans and investments of weekly reporting banks, trends in Reserve Bank credit, money rates, money in circulation, gold movements, interest rates in the United States as compared with those in major foreign countries, and a review of the economic situation in Europe. Unfortunately, progress in developing, interpreting, and analyzing statistical material outpaced its use by System officials.[3]

FOREIGN OPERATIONS

Establishment and development of relations between the Federal Reserve System and foreign central banks was given consideration both by the Board and the presidents of the Reserve Banks in the early years of the System. There was general agreement that establishment of such relationships was desirable and in the public interest.

Early in the twenties there was renewed consideration of foreign operations and the role the Federal Reserve System should play in helping restore international financial stability. Memoranda were prepared in 1923, for example, reviewing foreign operations of central banks and analyzing the role the Federal Reserve System might play. It was pointed out that prior

---

[3] A secondary use of material developed in the research program was publication of a national summary of business conditions prepared by the Board's staff, and monthly reviews prepared by the Reserve Banks. The purposes of these publications were frequently discussed at meetings of System officials. The consensus was that the publications should present a factual review of business and credit developments nationally and in the Reserve Districts. There were differences of opinion as to whether these publications should serve as a means of informing the public of the functions and operations of the Federal Reserve System. Some were vigorously opposed to any attempt to explain current Federal Reserve policy on the basis that "too many spokesmen" would lead to confusion. Others, especially some Reserve Bank presidents, thought the monthly reviews could make a useful contribution by explaining some of the problems confronting the Federal Reserve and the policies it was pursuing.

to the war, central banks tried to exercise a stabilizing influence on foreign exchanges, the flow of gold, and the volume of credit. The central bank would usually acquire a portfolio of foreign bills on gold standard countries when foreign exchange rates were at a low level. When the rate moved up, the central bank could sell some of its holdings of foreign bills and thereby prevent or retard gold exports. The general feeling was that the Federal Reserve Banks should continue close relations with important foreign central banks. It was also agreed that more effective control over gold movements and foreign exchange rates could be achieved by cooperation among central banks than by transacting business through private banks.

The Federal Reserve System, especially the President of the Federal Reserve Bank of New York, played a leading role in working out arrangements in the twenties to help foreign countries stabilize their currencies and return to the gold standard. Some of the techniques employed were a forerunner of recent operations of the Federal Reserve and the Treasury in defending the dollar.

The Federal Reserve System extended credit to several foreign central banks to assist foreign countries to stabilize their exchange rates and to facilitate their return to the gold standard. The largest amount was the arrangement with the Bank of England. In 1925, the Federal Reserve Bank of New York entered into an agreement, to run for two years, to furnish the Bank of England up to a total at any one time of $200 million of gold. If any part of the $200 million were used, the Bank of England agreed to give the Federal Reserve Bank of New York a credit on its books in sterling for the equivalent of the dollars used. A portion or all of this balance credited to the Federal Reserve Bank of New York might be invested from time to time in eligible sterling bills and held for the Reserve Bank's account. The interest rate charged the Bank of England for the amount of credit used was to be 1 per cent above the discount rate of the Federal Reserve Bank of New York for 90-day commercial paper; however, the rate should not be less than 4 per cent or more than 6 per cent. If the discount rate of the Federal Reserve Bank of New York should go above 6 per cent, the Bank of England would then pay the discount rate. The Federal Reserve was protected against loss by a provision that the exact amount of dollars in terms of gold furnished the Bank of England should be repaid in dollars in New York plus interest at the agreed rate. The British Government also guaranteed the obligation of the Bank of England to repay. The arrangement was approved by the Board of Governors, and all of the Reserve Banks agreed to participate. As it turned out, no part of the $200 million credit was actually used.

Arrangements were made with several foreign central banks whereby the System agreed to purchase from them up to certain amounts of prime commercial bills. The System also engaged in foreign exchange transactions at times. If properly timed, purchases or sales in small amounts would provide a stabilizing influence on exchange rates and exert some influence on the inflow and outflow of gold. In influencing gold flows, these transactions were considered as a supplement to—not a substitute for—changes in the discount rate. Foreign exchange operations were considered an especially useful supplement to the discount rate at times when an increase in the rate sufficient to check a gold outflow might raise interest rates, cause a sharp contraction of credit, and thus have serious adverse effects on the domestic economy.

4. PIONEERING IN POLICY: USE OF THE TOOLS

It should be remembered that the injection of Reserve Bank funds into the money market [by open market purchases] acts as a stimulant to it and the resale of such securities has the reverse effect.

—*Open Market Investment Committee, 1923*

Along with goals and guides, considerable thought was given to how the tools might best be used to achieve System objectives. Early in the twenties, officials recognized there were two channels through which Federal Reserve funds could be supplied to the market. The discount window supplied funds at the initiative of borrowing member banks. Open market operations supplied or absorbed funds at the initiative of the System.

The discount rate and discount policy were the means of influencing the flow of funds through the discount window; in fact, these were the only methods of regulating the flow of credit that were considered prior to the twenties. Open market operations, initiated to help develop a market for bankers acceptances and to bolster Reserve Bank earnings, soon came to be recognized as a significant instrument of Federal Reserve policy. Papers were prepared by officials and discussed at policy meetings as to use of the discount rate, open market operations, and coordination of these twin instruments.

DISCOUNT RATE

Discount rate discussions dealt mainly with the desirability of preferential rates, effects of discount rate changes, and effectiveness of the discount rate as compared with discretion in administering the discount window.

Preferential rates

Federal Reserve officials had established a preferential discount rate on Government securities to facilitate Treasury financing during the war. At times, a preferential rate had been used to encourage the development and use of certain types of paper.

In 1923, the Under Secretary of the Treasury proposed a preferential discount rate on Treasury certificates and bankers acceptances. He contended that paper which had acquired a regular status in the open market should have a preferential rate over ordinary customer loans of commercial banks. Inasmuch as the Treasury had been trying to develop a market for its certificates and the Reserve Banks had been trying to broaden the market for bankers acceptances, preferential rates would help promote a broader market for both, and would encourage banks to adjust their reserve positions in the market, leaving Reserve Banks with only marginal demands to be met.

Federal Reserve officials were generally opposed to the Under Secretary's proposal. Experience demonstrated that a preferential rate becomes the effective discount rate because member banks use paper carrying the lowest rate. Several were opposed as a matter of principle. A uniform discount rate for all types of paper was considered desirable in order that all member banks have access to Reserve Bank credit at the same rate. Unless justified by some unusual situation such as war, a preferential rate was a form of discrimination inconsistent with the public functions of the Federal Reserve System. Preferential rates on certificates and acceptances would also tend to discriminate against country banks because customarily only city banks held these types of short-term paper. In a vote taken at a presidents' conference, only one president favored the Treasury proposal.

A preferential discount rate was thus rejected as an instrument of policy, its use being confined to facilitating Treasury financing during a war.

Effects of rate changes

Widespread criticism that the Federal Reserve was to blame for the depression of 1920-1921 was still vivid in the minds of policymakers. Even though they believed deflation and depression were an inevitable aftermath of the war, they were anxious to avoid a recurrence. This was undoubtedly a motive in taking a careful look at the effects of changes in the discount rate. Two main lines of thought developed as to effectiveness of rate changes.

One view was that the discount rate was relatively ineffective in regulating the volume of discounts and advances to a member bank. In the United States it was impractical to keep the discount rate above the lending rate banks charged customers. Consequently, the rate was no real deterrent to borrowing. Neither was reduction in the rate effective in retarding or checking liquidation. Once under way, liquidation would continue until there was general expectation that prices would not go lower. Reserve Banks would have to rely mainly on discretion to prevent excessive borrowing by member banks. The principal value of the discount rate was not in regulating discounting at Reserve Banks but as a signal of official opinion as to anticipated credit demand. An increase in the discount rate, for example, served as a precautionary signal which in turn tended to cause banks to be more careful in making loans to their customers.

The opposing view was that the discount rate as a cost does influence the volume of member borrowing. Even though the rate is typically below bank-loan rates to customers it represents the cost of obtaining additional Reserve Bank credit. An increase in cost tends to discourage member-bank borrowing, whereas a decrease encourages borrowing. In the opinion of some presidents, experience demonstrated this was true.

An even more important argument was that discretion could not be relied on to regulate total volume of credit for the country as a whole. In a period of expansion, each loan application received by member banks might well have the appearance of a proper demand for credit. Approving only those loans which appeared to be for legitimate purposes would not result in appropriate control of the total volume of credit. The same problem arises in using discretionary control of the discount window by the Reserve Banks.[1]

---

[1] In debating effectiveness of the discount rate at the annual joint conference of the three policymaking groups in the fall of 1922, two officials with opposing views referred to their correspondence with a "well-known and highly esteemed" professor in one of the leading universities in support of their positions. It turned out that both had been corresponding with the same professor.

These divergent views on the discount rate reflected two fundamental and related differences: the individual bank versus the banking system, and use versus quantity of credit. Those favoring discretion approached the problem from the standpoint of regulating borrowing by an individual member bank. The discount rate was ineffective for this purpose because it was typically below bank lending rates. And if ineffective for individual banks it was also ineffective in regulating total credit.

Those favoring the discount rate were thinking mainly in terms of the banking system and aggregate credit. Admitting that discretion was sometimes essential to prevent excessive borrowing by individual member banks, it was not a suitable means of regulating total credit because even if extension of credit were confined to legitimate uses, the total might still become excessive in relation to physical output. Lurking underneath was the old controversy of use versus quantity as an appropriate goal of credit policy.

In the fall of 1927, a survey was made as to the effects of a change in the discount rate on loan rates member banks charged their customers. Several Reserve Banks sent out letters and questionnaires to all of their member banks; others checked through their bank relations men calling on member banks. The results indicated that a change in discount rate had no noticeable effect on customer loan rates of country banks. There was usually some effect on rates of larger banks, especially rates closely tied to market rates, such as brokers' loans, stock-market loans, and rates on acceptances. Apparently, a change in the discount rate was often used by large borrowers to negotiate a lower rate; they would threaten to borrow elsewhere unless the bank reduced its rate. Respondents reported an increase in the discount rate sometimes resulted in a fairly prompt rise in customer rates charged by large city banks.

DISCOUNT POLICY

Discount policy was often used with reference to principles governing administration of the discount window. Despite differences of opinion as to whether discretion was an effective means of regulating total volume of credit, there was agreement that it should be used to prevent excessive borrowing by individual banks.

Many member banks continued to borrow heavily from the Reserve Banks in the early twenties, not infrequently to carry Government securities acquired in War Loan and Victory Loan drives. This large volume of member-bank borrowing focused attention on discount policy.

In the fall of 1923, a "go-around" revealed that most Reserve Banks kept close watch on borrowing, especially member banks that borrowed excessively. Some Reserve Banks still used a basic line calculated for each member bank as a guide, scrutinizing more carefully banks borrowing in excess of this line. One Federal Reserve Bank adjusted its loans to member banks for seasonal variation to get some idea of whether banks were borrowing more than their normal seasonal requirements. Practically all of the Reserve Banks tried to keep informed as to reasons for borrowing, use to be made of the proceeds, financial condition of borrowers, and similar information. Most Reserve Banks relied on direct methods rather than the discount rate to regulate borrowing of individual member banks. As one Reserve Bank official stated, it was necessary to treat each case individually, "we must treat the patient in the bed and not in the book."

Professor Sprague of Harvard University was asked to make a study of member-bank borrowing, and submitted a report in the fall of 1925. He reported a large number of member banks still borrowing as a result of what happened in 1918 to 1920. One of the problems was to educate member-bank officials as to appropriate borrowing from a Reserve Bank. He suggested that officials emphasize that using Reserve Bank credit to supplement a bank's own capital is not appropriate.

There was general agreement that borrowing to meet seasonal and other temporary or emergency needs was appropriate; borrowing to take advantage of a rate differential or continuous borrowing to supplement a bank's own resources was not.

OPEN MARKET OPERATIONS

A major step in the decade of the twenties was the development of open market operations as an instrument of monetary policy.

The significance of this tool was discovered largely accidentally. As discounts and advances declined in 1921 as a result of the depression, the Reserve Banks began buying Government securities to bolster earnings. But it soon became apparent that these purchases were having significant monetary effects, and that open market operations should be governed by policy considerations— not by earnings.

Early goals and guides

Once open market operations were considered a tool of monetary policy, discussion turned toward the purposes for which this new tool should be used. By the latter part of 1923, a twofold objective had emerged. First, they should be used to help stabilize the business situation by putting additional funds into the market when business liquidation is going too fast, and withdrawing funds when business is too active or speculative. Second, open market operations were a suitable tool for offsetting seasonal stringencies, and other temporary disturbing forces such as Treasury operations at tax-payment dates.

These objectives in turn focused attention on information that would be helpful in determining when and in what quantity purchases and sales should be made in the market. One of the major guides for open market operations in the twenties was the reserve position of member banks, especially the money-market banks in New York City. Movements of funds through the market were sooner or later reflected in reserve positions of the money-market banks. The Federal Reserve Bank of New York watched reserve positions closely, making an hourly tabulation of the more important factors affecting them. Among the factors included in reserve estimates were wire transfers, clearing-house balances, exports and imports of gold, and inflows and outflows of currency. These estimates and other information provided a reasonably good indication of whether the New York money market was likely to have a net gain or net loss of reserves for the day.

A second indicator of conditions in the money market was the call-loan rate. This was a sensitive rate because money-market banks used the call-loan market to adjust their reserve positions. When short of reserves, banks called loans, thus forcing the rate up. When they had excess reserves, they were anxious to make new loans and the call-loan rate tended to decline. |

| Another guide followed in the twenties was borrowing by member banks, especially in the principal financial centers such as New York and Chicago.| A report of the Open Market Investment Committee in 1926, for example, stated that experience had shown that when member banks in New York City were borrowing $100 million or more, there was real pressure for reducing loans. But when borrowings were negligible the money market was usually easy, with market rates dropping below the discount rate.| Other guides referred to in the twenties were the general level of interest rates and movement of foreign exchange rates, the latter indicating the probability of gold imports or exports. |

Recommendations of the Open Market Investment Committee were usually in quantitative terms. For example, in the fall of 1923 the Committee recommended purchases up to $100 million. There was some preference for conducting operations in short-term securities because their prices fluctuated in a much narrower range than longer-term securities.

Effects of open market operations

As with the discount rate, System officials tried to determine the effects of open market operations. Were the effects limited to financial centers or did they spread throughout the country? Most of the presidents thought they had some effect in their districts. The first effect was likely to be a reduction in borrowing from the Reserve Bank. Lower rates and easier credit, initially in New York City where the bulk of the purchases was concentrated, made borrowing in the market more attractive to large business firms. This put downward pressure on bank rates in the large financial centers and then tended to spread to other cities. As one official summed it up in 1926, the effects were felt first and with the greatest impact in the financial centers, and then spread over the country with diminishing intensity. |

| A few officials thought open market operations had certain advantages over the discount rate. They had the advantage of being more flexible and therefore could be used at times when an increase in the discount rate might be too drastic. Open market

operations were not followed by the public and hence had less psychological impact than a change in the discount rate. Because of these advantages, some thought open market operations were a suitable tool for probing the market when evidence was not yet sufficient for a definite and overt move toward restraint or ease.

A member of the Board of Governors had serious reservations about open market operations. He thought this tool should be reserved for "rare occasions" when its use was necessary. Reserves supplied by open market operations were much more likely to be misused than reserves supplied through the discount window. Purchases release funds to the market without any restrictions as to use. Initially, the funds go mainly to money-market banks and unless business demand is sufficient to absorb them, the banks put the funds into the call-loan market. In his opinion supplying reserves when business demand for credit is slack is practically an invitation for banks to use them for speculative purposes. He thought open market purchases in 1927, by creating excess funds which banks put into call loans, provided the basis for the subsequent speculative stock-market boom.

In contrast to open market operations, reserves supplied through the discount window are in response to a demand. Moreover, most member banks are reluctant to borrow from a Reserve Bank and therefore are unlikely to do so in order to make speculative loans. For this reason, he thought reserves supplied through the discount window were much less likely to be misused than reserves supplied by open market operations.

Centralization and supervision

Effective use of open market operations as a tool of monetary policy was seriously handicapped by decentralized control. Officials soon recognized that purchases and sales of Government securities would have to be centralized and coordinated.

In a sense the initial step was taken in October, 1920, when the Conference of Presidents of the Reserve Banks appointed a standing committee to study and keep informed on market conditions and practices in bankers acceptances. The committee was expected to develop uniform practices and policies for the Reserve Banks, suggest buying rates and, in general, work toward broadening and developing an open market for acceptances. The committee appointed a secretary who had an office in the Federal Reserve Bank of New York. Each Reserve Bank telegraphed a weekly report to the secretary, giving information on rates at which the Reserve Bank had purchased bills, the amount purchased, the amount of repurchase agreements and rates at which they were negotiated, and the general demand and supply situation for acceptances in its district.

In 1922, the Conference of Presidents established a committee on centralized execution of purchases and sales of Government securities. The committee originally consisted of the Presidents of the Federal Reserve Banks of Boston, Philadelphia, Chicago, and New York, and later the President of the Federal Reserve Bank of Cleveland was added.

There were two main reasons for establishment of the committee. An important one was a vigorous complaint by Treasury officials that the Reserve Banks were creating artificial conditions in the Government securities market and thus making Treasury financing more difficult. In fact, Treasury officials wanted the Reserve Banks gradually to dispose of the Governments they had acquired and get out of the market altogether. A second reason was that Reserve Banks were competing against each other. Most of the purchases were made in New York City because it was the principal money-market center. The committee's task was to develop more orderly procedures and bring about better coordination of purchases in order not to interfere with Treasury operations and to avoid competition among the Reserve Banks. The Federal Reserve Bank of New York was designated to make purchases and sales, purchases being allocated among participating Reserve Banks according to an agreed formula.

Even though Reserve Bank officials recognized the need for centralized operations, they were unwilling to give up the right of the Reserve Bank to buy and sell for its own account. Practically all Reserve Bank presidents insisted that ultimate decision as to purchase or sale of securities rested with the board of directors of each Reserve Bank. In October, 1922, the committee entered the field of policy, with approval of the presidents, by making recommendations to the Reserve Banks as to the advisability of purchases or sales. In order not to interfere with Treasury financing, the committee urged the Reserve Banks to stay out of the market when the Federal Reserve Bank of New York was executing orders for Treasury account and during a Treasury financing or refunding operation.

In 1923, the Board of Governors abolished the committee formed in 1922 and established the Open Market Investment Committee with the same membership, under the supervision of the Board. The Board laid down certain principles that should govern open market operations. First, the time, manner, character, and volume of such operations by the Reserve Banks should be governed "with primary regard to the accommodation of commerce and business, and to the effect of such purchases or sales on the general credit situation." Second, in selecting open market purchases, careful regard should be given to the effect on the market for Government securities. Except for repurchase agreements in Treasury certificates, the Board recommended that purchases be mainly in eligible commercial paper. In November, 1923, at the request of the Federal Reserve Bank of New York and with approval of the Board of Governors, the Open Market Investment Committee took over supervision of foreign transactions to help promote a uniform policy.

The new committee was a step forward in centralization of open market operations. The procedure was for the Open Market Investment Committee to meet and make recommendations as to open market policy. Recommendations were then submitted to the Board of Governors for approval. Once approved by the Board, each Reserve Bank still reserved the right to participate or not to participate in the recommended operations. Essentially, this same procedure continued until the Open Market Committee was completely reorganized under the Banking Act of 1935. The problem which lingered on into the twenties was the Reserve Banks insisting on their right to buy and sell long-term Government securities as needed for earnings and to execute transactions with member banks in their districts. Practically all Reserve Bank officials recognized, however, that such transactions tended to nullify the work of the Open Market Investment Committee, and the volume was not significant after 1924.

The Chairman of the Board of Governors suggested in the fall of 1928 that the Open Market Investment Committee be discontinued and an Open Market Policy Conference, consisting of a representative from each Reserve Bank selected annually by the board of directors, be established in its place. No action was taken, however, until the spring of 1930, when a joint meeting of the Open Market Investment Committee (including informally representatives from all of the Reserve Banks) with the Board agreed that the Open Market Investment Committee should be discontinued. An Open Market Policy Conference, consisting of a representative from each Reserve Bank, was established in its place.

The Conference was to meet with the Board of Governors at the call of the Chairman of the Board, who was also Chairman of the Conference. The primary function of the Open Market Policy Conference was to develop and recommend policies and plans with regard to open market operations. The recommendations of the Conference, if approved by the Board, were to be submitted to the Reserve Banks. Any Reserve Bank dissenting from the recommended policy was expected to give its reasons to the Board and the Chairman of the Executive Committee of the Policy Conference.

An Executive Committee of five members was given power to act in the execution of policies recommended by the Open Market Policy Conference and approved by the Board of Governors. The Executive Committee appointed for the first year consisted of the President of the Federal Reserve Bank of New York as Chairman and representatives (actually presidents) of the Federal Reserve Banks of Boston, Philadelphia, Cleveland, and Chicago.

Repurchase agreements

Use of repurchase agreements with dealers was approved by the Board of Governors, both as to legality and principle, in 1921 and again in 1925. The agreements were usually for a maturity of up to 15 days.

Initially, repurchase agreements were used to help dealers carry an inventory of acceptances and securities in times of stringency when credit was not available from the usual sources at reasonable rates. The ultimate objective was to encourage development of the market for acceptances. By the mid-twenties, however, repurchase agreements were being used as a tool of monetary policy—a convenient method of supplying funds to the market temporarily.

RESERVE REQUIREMENTS

In the twenties, reserve requirements were thought of primarily as a means of increasing the safety of deposits. But as early as 1923, one official stated the real function of reserve requirements was to prevent too much credit expansion.

A Reserve Bank official proposed a revision in 1925 that would have made reserve requirements a means of influencing credit expansion and contraction. He suggested that the requirement be divided into two parts: a certain percentage against demand and time deposits, and a certain percentage of the banks' indebtedness to the Reserve Banks. The requirement against borrowing from the Reserve Bank would be levied on a graduated scale, the percentage rising as the proportion of borrowing to the member bank's capital increased. For example, the requirement might be 10 per cent when borrowing is 50 to 100 per cent of the bank's capital, rising to 50 per cent when borrowing is 400 to 500 per cent of capital. He thought this plan would correct a shortcoming of fixed reserve requirements in that it would automatically tend to restrain overexpansion in a boom and encourage expansion in a recession.

The search for some method of curbing speculative use of credit with a minimum of harmful effects on business led to a proposal in 1928 that the Board of Governors be given authority to raise reserve requirements for member banks in reserve and central reserve cities. Some officials thought raising reserve requirements in reserve and central reserve cities would hit most of the banks making stock-exchange loans.

COORDINATION AND TIMING

As the monetary effects of open market operations were recognized, the question arose as to how this new tool might best be coordinated with the discount rate. Most of the thinking was in terms of exercising restraint. Stabilization in the early twenties was visualized mainly as a problem of preventing an inflationary boom. This was also considered the best means of avoiding the depression which would inevitably follow.

Proper coordination of open market operations and the discount rate could provide more effective restraint than either used separately. Open market operations, which the public did not regard as a signal of System intentions, were useful for probing the market to get some idea of the strength of credit demands. This tool was also more suitable than the discount rate for making an initial move pending clearer evidence of a need for more or less restraint. A tentative decision that more restraint was probably desirable could be implemented by selling securities, absorbing reserves, and forcing member banks into the discount window to borrow. Once it became clear that further restraint was needed, the discount rate could be increased. And the increase would be more effective because banks were having to borrow. Some suggested the opposite sequence—raise the discount rate and then follow with sales of securities to make it effective. This sequence was based on the belief that open market operations were more effective than a change in the discount rate.

For instance, open market operations were used to probe the strength of credit demands in the latter part of 1922 and in 1923 when prices were moving upward. According to a member of the Board of Governors, officials were uncertain as to whether the price rise reflected only a natural readjustment following the sharp decline in the depression of 1920–1921. To test the situation, securities were sold to take funds out of the market. The resulting increase in member-bank borrowing from the Reserve Banks was regarded as evidence that the volume of credit in use was needed, at least in the judgment of member banks. Some thought member banks would not borrow from the Reserve Banks to make speculative loans. A second effect of the open market sale of securities was to put member banks in a position so that the discount rate would be more effective.

Coordinated use of these twin instruments was also believed to be more effective in depression than either used separately. Open market purchases, by putting additional funds into the market, had a direct stimulating effect on business activity. The funds supplied also enabled member banks to pay off some of their debts to the Reserve Banks. Because of member-bank reluctance to be in debt at the Reserve Bank, debt reduction might increase their willingness to lend more than lowering the discount rate.

Another type of coordination discussed related to purposes for which funds were supplied. Borrowing at the discount window might be used to meet seasonal needs, with open market operations being used to offset temporary deficiencies and surpluses. Open market purchases might also be used to supply some of the reserves needed to support credit expansion required by economic growth.

Proper timing was soon recognized as an important aspect of using the tools effectively. There was considerable discussion of the importance of timing in the early twenties. One official said it had been a common and painful observation to hear that a certain action would have been proper had it been taken three or four months ago. In his opinion, blunders and mistakes of the past were often due to System officials being doubtful and uncertain, which in turn resulted in part from a complex organization and fairly wide diffusion of responsibility. Uncertainty as to one's responsibility contributes to hesitation.

Timing of restrictive action was believed to be especially important in combatting inflation. This same official stressed that inflation is an insidious process; it does not begin as inflation but develops and grows into it. He stated: "If you wait with action in the matter of credit expansion until you see signs clearly that the development of inflation is unmistakable, then you have over-waited." There was general agreement that prompt action was likely to be much more effective.

"BETWEEN THE DEVIL AND THE DEEP SEA"

A dilemma began to emerge in the mid-twenties which was to frustrate and preoccupy officials for the remainder of the decade. The flow of credit into the stock market and growing speculation began to arouse official concern as early as 1925. Widespread criticism that the Federal Reserve had allowed credit expansion to get out of hand following the war—even though System officials thought for good reasons—created a strong desire to avoid a similar thing happening again. Hence there was a general inclination to try to nip speculation in the bud as soon as it emerged. But officials were confronted with a situation calling for conflicting actions. There was no boom in business activity. In fact, production was well below capacity, and agriculture which had suffered severe deflation in the postwar depression was again experiencing declining prices. |

| Thus the dilemma confronting policymakers: tighten credit and raise interest rates to discourage speculation with resulting adverse effects on business and agriculture, or ease credit and lower interest rates to bolster agriculture and business activity with the resulting risk of encouraging speculation. This was the situation that led a Reserve Bank president to state to a Congressional committee in 1926: "There you are, between the devil and the deep sea."

Officials were agreed as to the twofold goal they should strive for: to curb the flow of credit into speculative uses without making it scarcer and more expensive for business and agricultural purposes. But there was sharp disagreement as to action that should be taken.

One group, which included a majority of the Board of Governors, strongly favored direct pressure in administration of the discount window. Three main arguments were given in favor of this method. First, use of credit for speculative activities of any kind was clearly contrary to the intent of the Federal Reserve Act that Reserve Bank credit should be restricted to productive uses in industry, commerce, and agriculture. Second, effective regulation of the quality or proper use of credit would automatically result in the right quantity, thus avoiding booms and depressions. Third, raising the discount rate high enough to curb the flow of credit into the stock market would almost immediately precipitate a crisis with harmful effects on business and agriculture. In fact, the majority of the Board of Governors thought that by 1929 the call-loan rate was so high and speculation so rampant that the discount rate could no longer be used effectively. The only effective method of curbing speculation without hurting legitimate business was to refuse advances to member banks using the proceeds for speculative loans. For these reasons, the Board refused to approve recommendations for an increase in the discount rate made weekly by the Federal Reserve Bank of New York during the period February 14 to May 23, 1929.

Another group disagreed with the selective approach both on theoretical and practical grounds. Misuse of credit, such as for speculative activities, was only a part of the problem. Too much credit regardless of pattern of use could lead to a boom and inflation. Direct pressure was impractical because the use member banks make of borrowed reserves could not be determined. Even if the initial use of borrowed reserves could be regulated, subsequent uses could not. An illustration often given was that an advance might be made to a member bank with no security loans, but ordinary commercial transactions might shift the reserves to member banks making large amounts of speculative loans. Neither would careful examination of a member bank's loan portfolio accurately reveal customer use of loan proceeds. Loans made against securities did not necessarily indicate use of credit to purchase or carry securities. Such loans were often for business purposes. Hence attempts to regulate use of credit for speculation without restricting it for other purposes were doomed to failure.

The dilemma together with these widely divergent views of how best to deal with it led to a policy of watchful waiting. Speculative activity gathered momentum and attracted an ever-increasing flow of credit into the stock market. The System began imposing modest restraint early in 1928 through sales of securities and higher discount rates. In the late summer of 1928, the Board suggested a preferential discount rate for agricultural paper and a preferential buying rate for bankers acceptances in order to facilitate the marketing of farm products and help cushion the restrictive impact on agriculture. But because of strong opposition, especially by presidents of the Reserve Banks, the preferential discount rate was not established. In the late summer of 1929, System officials again tried to soften the impact of growing restraint on agriculture and business by buying bills in the open market to provide reserves to meet increased demand for credit during the crop-marketing season. With the same objective in mind, it was agreed that the Federal Reserve Bank of New York should increase its discount rate from 5 to 6 per cent, but increases at the other Reserve Banks should be delayed until after the seasonal credit demands of agriculture and business had been met.

5. THE GREAT DEPRESSION

Very large loans at very high rates are the best remedy for the worst malady of the money market when a foreign drain is added to a domestic drain.

— Walter Bagehot

The decade of the thirties was less productive than the twenties in the development of central banking theory and techniques. Federal Reserve officials were burdened and preoccupied with two major problems—a severe financial crisis and depression in the early thirties, and economic stagnation and huge excess reserves in the latter half of the decade.

Officials manifested grave concern over the depression, increasingly so as evidence began to emerge indicating that the country might be in the throes of an unusually severe deflation and decline in business activity. The developing situation and the implications for Federal Reserve policy were the principal topics of discussion at the meetings of policy groups throughout the depression period. Official records leave no doubt of a dedicated desire to pursue a policy that would contribute to sound business recovery. On the whole, analysis and diagnosis of the business and financial situation were good except that the severity of the decline was not anticipated, especially in its early stages. There was also fairly general agreement as to what was happening. But as to causes of the depression and what the Federal Reserve should do to help bring about recovery, disagreement soon developed.

A policy of passive ease to facilitate orderly liquidation and readjustments was favored by one group, consisting mainly of Reserve Bank presidents. For various reasons they opposed aggressive ease to *promote* recovery. Others, particularly a few members of the Board of Governors and the president of one of the Reserve Banks, favored a policy of more active ease. They thought that sooner or later a plentiful supply of funds and low rates would take hold and help stimulate recovery in business activity.

Federal Reserve policy during the depression passed through three general stages.[1] In the first stage, from the stock market crash to the spring of 1932, the principal aim was to make credit available at reasonable rates to help cushion deflation. In the second stage, from the spring of 1932 to the spring of 1933, amendment of the Federal Reserve Act to make Government securities eligible as collateral against Federal Reserve notes ushered in a more aggressive open market policy directed toward building up substantial excess reserves to induce credit expansion and stimulate business. In the third and final stage, the objectives were to maintain large excess reserves and to cooperate with the Government's national recovery program.

PASSIVE EASE

When the speculative bubble burst in the fall of 1929, there was a consensus that sharp liquidation in the stock market was a serious threat to business stability, especially since there were already some indications of a possible recession.

Ready availability of credit

The initial response, generally favored by policymakers, was two-fold. First, the System should do "all within its power" to assure the ready availability of credit for business purposes at reasonable rates. Acceptances and, if necessary, Government securities should be purchased to avoid any increase and possibly to bring some reduction in member-bank indebtedness to the Reserve Banks. Second, the Reserve Banks should follow a liberal discount and lending policy to member banks during the emergency situation. In conformity with the policy of making credit readily avail-

---

[1] In view of the interests of students of central banking in this period of monetary history, policy views are given in somewhat more detail and the chronological order of their development is adhered to more closely than in the remainder of the study.

able, holdings of Government securities and acceptances rose about $450 million in the last quarter of 1929. The increase seems small in terms of current magnitudes, but in relation to required reserves was roughly equivalent to an increase of about $4 billion at the present time. The discount rate was also reduced.

For the first few months, policy formulation was on the basis of an ordinary recession. In late January, 1930, the Board of Governors arranged a joint meeting with the presidents of the Reserve Banks. The consensus was that business was in a recession, the extent or duration of which could not then be determined. The panicky feeling manifested earlier had subsided. Funds had been made available, market rates were lower, and liquidation was progressing in an orderly way. As to policy, there was general agreement that any firming of rates should be prevented, but more ease was not desirable. The majority thought it would not be effective to try to stimulate business when it was in a downward trend. In their view it would not be desirable "to exhaust our ammunition now in what may be perhaps a vain attempt to stem an inevitable recession."

Disagreement over policy

The depression took a more serious turn than was anticipated early in 1930. The consensus, following a careful review of the situation in the latter part of May, was that business, agriculture, and trade were seriously depressed both here and abroad. As for policy, developments should be watched very carefully and the System should be prepared to act promptly if conditions warranted.

The worsening business and credit situation provoked a basic disagreement over policy in mid-1930 which continued during most of the depression. A small majority of the Board of Governors and Reserve Bank presidents favored buying up to $25 million of Government securities each week in the first two weeks of June. The aim was to make funds somewhat more readily available in the hope that it might encourage new business undertakings and thereby increase demand for surplus products overhanging the market. In the latter part of June the Executive Committee of the Open Market Policy Conference rejected by a four to one vote the Chairman's proposal that purchases of Government securities at about $25 million a week be continued.[2]

The group favoring somewhat more ease thought that inasmuch as the situation was getting worse instead of better, the System should do everything possible to establish easy money conditions favorable to business recovery. Discount rates and the buying rate on acceptances had been sharply reduced. The discount rate of the Federal Reserve Bank of New York had been lowered from 6 per cent in the fall of 1929 to 2½ per cent by the latter part of June. Short-term market rates had also declined sharply, rates on prime commercial paper and call loans having dropped from 6¼ per cent and 8.6 per cent, respectively, in September, 1929, to 3.5 per cent and 2.6 per cent in June, 1930. Believing that the supply of short-term funds was ample and at low rates, additional open market purchases was the most promising step available to the System. One possible benefit of buying more Government securities was an improved bond market, an increased flow of capital funds to business, and more purchasing power for the surplus supply of commodities on the market. Under existing conditions, there was no danger that the further ease contemplated would stimulate a revival of speculation. In short, moderate purchases of Governments would not do any harm and it might do some good.

There was substantial opposition to the proposed program of additional open market purchases, based largely on the theory that the depression was the result mainly of nonmonetary causes such as overproduction and excess capacity in a number of industries. Therefore, cheaper and more abundant credit would not stimulate business recovery. Instead, more ease might encourage increases in productive capacity, defer essential readjustments, and retard recovery. This view was well stated in a memorandum submitted to the Open Market Policy Conference in September, 1930, by a Reserve Bank president. According to the memorandum:

---

[2] The Open Market Policy Conference, composed of a representative (actually the president) of each Reserve Bank, resulted from reorganization of the Open Market Investment Committee. The Conference met with the Board of Governors, subject to the call of the Chairman of the Conference. The Executive Committee consisted of five members of the Conference.

If we understand the reasoning correctly, the policy of buying Government securities is justified by some argument as this—we are in a period of depression characterized by falling commodity prices and a deplorable volume of unemployment. This condition cannot be corrected without an increase of building activity. Building activity will be brought about by low rates for long-time loans. Low rates for long-time loans will only come with a strong and active bond market. Therefore we should bring about this condition of the bond market by making short-time credit so cheap that banks and investors will be driven to the bond market to utilize their funds. . . .

This over-production did not manifest itself until a year ago, because, under the stimulus of instalment selling and an unreasoning belief in long-continued and unprecedented prosperity, over-buying kept pace with over-production. The consequences of such an economic debauch are inevitable. We are now suffering them.

Can they be corrected by cheap money? We do not believe they can. We believe that the correction must come about through reduced production, reduced inventories, the gradual reduction of consumer credit, the liquidation of security loans, and the accumulation of savings through the exercise of thrift. These are slow and simple remedies, but just as there is 'no royal road to knowledge,' we believe that there is no shortcut or panacea for the rectification of existing conditions. We do entertain, however, the belief that the declines in commodity prices and in employment have about run their course, and that the foundations for business revival have already been laid.[3]

The president of another Reserve Bank advised the Board of Governors that his Bank did not want to participate in a recent purchase of $50 million of Government securities for the following reasons:

a. *With credit cheap and redundant we do not believe that business recovery will be accelerated by making credit cheaper and more redundant.*

b. *We find no reason to believe that excessively cheap money will promote or create a bond market, seeing evidence in the recent past to the contrary, and, further, do not consider the promotion or creation of a bond market one of the functions of the Federal Reserve System.*

c. *We believe there may come an opportune moment to put money into the market when that action will have a beneficial effect and feel that if, at such a time, our open market portfolio of Governments is excessive there may be hesitation to increase it.*[4]

---

[3] From a memorandum submitted to the Open Market Policy Conference, September 25, 1930.

[4] Letter to the Board of Governors, June 16, 1930.

Federal Reserve authorities kept close watch on the developing situation and became increasingly concerned as business and credit conditions continued to deteriorate. The memorandum submitted to the meeting of the Executive Committee of the Open Market Policy Conference in late December, 1930, analyzed the situation as follows: severe depression had continued with business activity still declining; a series of bank failures, especially the more spectacular ones, had shaken public confidence; declining bond prices had depreciated bank investment portfolios and impaired the capital of some banks, country banks being especially hard hit; there had been extraordinary demand for currency; many banks were dumping securities to get in a more liquid position, and banks generally were reluctant to make commitments except for very short term; and the bond market was almost completely closed to new issues.

Heavy deposit withdrawals were putting some banks under increasing strain. Early in 1931, one Reserve Bank president suggested that it would be desirable to give Reserve Banks authority to discount notes collateralled by listed bonds under proper safeguards in order that they could better assist banks encountering runs. Sometimes in such emergency situations Reserve Banks had bought Government securities directly from the banks; however, this was not consistent with the policy of centralized open market operations adopted by the Open Market Policy Conference and the Board of Governors.

Continued deterioration in the business and credit situation led to careful consideration of policy at the April, 1931, meeting of the Open Market Policy Conference. The Chairman's report to the Conference stated, with reference to open market operations since the stock market crash in the fall of 1929, they "were not pursued with the idea that thereby any vigorous stimulant might be given to business or finance, but rather with the idea of removing in a period of reaction and depression the pressure which had been placed upon the market in 1928 and 1929," especially by high interest rates and a restricted supply of funds.

Even though open market operations had not as yet been used mainly for the purpose of stimulating expansion, there was concern as to why gold imports had not had the usual expansionary effect on bank loans and investments expected under the gold standard. There were several obstacles to the desired expansionary effect:

> *An expansion of foreign lending requires that investors should be willing to purchase foreign bonds. An expansion of domestic commercial credit requires that businessmen should be willing to borrow. An expansion of long-term bank investments to provide capital which is in demand here and abroad, requires that banks which have recently taken huge losses in securities, and upon which the lesson of liquidity has been enforced by sad experience, should be willing to purchase bonds.*[5]

After extended discussion of what could be done in order that gold imports might have their traditional effect, a threefold program was agreed upon. The first step was a reduction in the bill-buying rate to as low as 1 per cent, if necessary, in order that the System could maintain or even increase its bill holdings despite gold imports which had totaled about $400 million in the past 15 months. Second, the reduction in the bill-buying rate should be followed shortly by a decrease in the discount rate. Third, if necessary, the System should resort to further purchases of Government securities.

It was hoped that this program would eventually encourage banks to expand their loans and investments. The Reserve Bank president who made the proposal stated that, "this policy sooner or later would necessarily, because of its effect upon the short-time money rates, encourage banks and depositors in banks, in spite of their present liquidity, to employ their money, which now is becoming relatively so unprofitable." The Open Market Policy Conference approved the program, and authorized the Executive Committee, if and when it appeared necessary or advisable, to purchase up to $100 million of Government securities.

The Conference of Presidents also recommended in April, 1931, that the Federal Reserve Act be amended so that in an emergency Reserve Banks could make advances to member banks on their own promissory notes secured by noneligible collateral. Such advances should be subject to rules and regulations prescribed by the Board of Governors, and the maturity should be limited to

---

[5] The Chairman's report to the Open Market Policy Conference, April 27, 1931.

15 days or less. The presidents favored this amendment in order that Reserve Banks would be better able to meet the credit needs of member banks, especially in cases of heavy deposit withdrawals.

By late summer of 1931, a series of financial disturbances at home and abroad were intensifying the financial crisis and the depression. A worldwide drop in commodity prices had thrown the international trade of many countries out of balance, increased the burden of foreign debts, and reduced national income. Foreign trade of the United States had been cut to less than one-half the 1929 total. Deposit withdrawals and bank failures continued. Member banks were striving for more liquidity and were not putting excess reserves to use. Officials thought the situation sufficiently serious to justify consideration of "every sound remedy." With the discount rate of the Federal Reserve Bank of New York at 1½ per cent, the market rate on prime commercial paper 2 per cent, and the call-loan rate 1½ per cent in August, 1931, about the only additional step available was open market purchases. Some favored substantial purchases even though growing lack of confidence might cause banks to hold the additional reserves as excess.

But opposition to purchases of Government securities was also growing. Some who had favored additional purchases thought that loss of confidence would likely cause member banks to hold the funds as excess reserves. Several presidents were becoming seriously concerned over the reserve position of their Reserve Banks. Because of runs and the internal drain on reserves, they thought the Reserve Banks should maintain a liquid position. Sudden demands by member banks might prove embarrassing if the System's resources were tied up in Government securities. Moreover, purchases of Government securities usually resulted in a reduction in member-bank discounting, and tended to impair the System's free gold position. A reduction in member-bank discounts meant less eligible paper available as collateral for Federal Reserve notes. With a shortage of eligible paper, Reserve Banks would have to substitute gold in order to issue Federal Reserve notes. Concern over their low and deteriorating reserve positions in the face of growing member-bank demands for currency and advances strengthened opposition to additional purchases of Government securities. Some Reserve Bank presidents, apprehensive about their dwindling reserves, refused to participate in further purchases. They put a higher priority on conserving their ability to meet emergency needs of member banks than on putting additional reserves in the market which, in their opinion, might be held as excess reserve anyway.

Restraint to meet financial crisis

The United States experienced an extraordinary financial crisis in the fall of 1931. Prices of U. S. Government securities dropped precipitately; bank failures increased; and banks were emphasizing liquidity. The securities markets were almost completely closed to new financing, and the banking situation constituted a serious obstacle to business recovery.

The internal crisis was complicated by an external drain as well as serious disruption of international trade and finance. The largest gold export movement in the country's history up to that time was combined with heavy domestic withdrawals of currency. The United States lost about $700 million of gold in the latter part of September and in October, but the ability of foreigners to get gold brought a rapid restoration of confidence in the dollar. As a result of the credit crisis, however, funds lay idle for want of reputable borrowers; purchasing power in international markets was curtailed; industrial countries ceased to buy desired quantities of foods and raw materials; and countries producing primary products were unable to buy manufactured goods.

Federal Reserve officials reacted to this acute credit crisis in the traditional way—increases in discount rates and a policy of lending freely. Walter Bagehot was quoted at length in support of this policy. His admonition (note the quotation at the beginning of the chapter) that a central bank facing both internal and external drains should lend freely but at high rates to discourage unnecessary borrowing was still widely accepted. The discount rate was raised to discourage unnecessary borrowing but more important perhaps to protect the gold reserve. There was general agreement that the gold standard should be maintained. Prompt action appeared necessary to halt the gold drain.

To implement the principle of lending freely, the consensus was that the Reserve Banks should pursue a liberal policy toward member banks in difficulty; such banks should be encouraged to borrow freely from the Reserve Banks when necessary to meet emergency situations. One official stated: "The present [is] a time when liquidity should be used rather than preserved."

Late in 1931, the gold outflow ceased and the demand for currency subsided somewhat. System officials, aware of the heavy deflation that had occurred and the severity of the depression gripping the country, explored what the Federal Reserve could do to prevent further deflation and help bring about some improvement in the business situation. In mid-January, 1932, it was agreed that the discount rate should be reduced; the System should cooperate fully with the Treasury in its borrowing program, estimated at $1.5 billion in the first half of the year; and Government securities should be purchased when desirable, not to exceed a total of $200 million.

Renewed outflow of gold and the declining free gold reserve position led System officials to defer carrying out this program. In late February, there was an extended discussion at a joint meeting of the Open Market Policy Conference and the Board of Governors of the desirability of moving ahead with the program agreed on in January. Some members of the Board and the president of one of the Reserve Banks were strongly in favor of purchasing Government securities. One Board member favored purchases on a larger scale than the program approved in January. He said there "was never a safer time to operate boldly than at present." But there was strong opposition, especially among the presidents. Apprehension over the dwindling free gold position swelled the ranks of the group opposed to open market purchases.

MORE ACTIVE EASE

Passage of the Glass-Steagall Act in February, 1932, ushered in a policy of more active ease. The System embarked on a program of substantial purchases of Government securities to build up excess reserves, which later was supplemented by efforts to encourage banks to put reserves to use. Discount rates were also reduced.

The Glass-Steagall Act, by relieving some of the anxiety over the System's gold reserve position, was an important factor leading to a more active open market policy. The Act permitted Government securities as collateral against Federal Reserve notes except for the 40 per cent minimum gold reserve requirement. The Reserve Banks were thus able to improve their gold reserve position by substituting Government securities for gold held as collateral in excess of the 40 per cent minimum requirement because of the shortage of eligible paper. The Act also permitted Reserve Banks to make advances to member banks against ineligible assets under certain conditions.

The program of purchasing Government securities was carefully reconsidered. Several officials thought the open market program had had at least limited success. With the improved gold reserve position, it was decided to initiate a more active open market policy. The objectives of enlarged purchases were "to check the unprecedented liquidation of bank credit which was exerting a seriously depressing influence on business and prices"; to "enable member banks to pay off indebtedness and accumulate some excess reserves," thus lessening the pressure for liquidation; and to "exert some influence in the direction of a recovery in business and in commodity and in bond prices." From the end of February to the middle of July, 1932, System holdings of Governments rose over $1 billion.

The immediate target of open market operations shifted from a certain quantity of purchases to building up and maintaining excess reserves.[6] In June, 1932, it was agreed that open market policy should be directed toward maintaining excess reserves of between $250–300 million. Purchases should also be timed so that System holdings of Governments would show some increase from week to week in order to avoid any uncertainty on the part of the public as to whether the program had been changed. Actually, excess reserves averaged about $270 million in the third quarter

---

[6] Ease of implementation was one reason for changing the directive to maintaining a certain amount of excess reserves; otherwise a telephone conference of the Executive Committee was often necessary to decide on the amount to be purchased each week.

of 1932 and nearly $500 million in the fourth quarter—equivalent, in terms of required reserves, to excess reserves at present of over $3 billion and $5 billion, respectively.

Officials realized that success of the enlarged open market program would depend on use of excess reserves by member banks. Several methods of encouraging use of reserves were discussed, such as national and regional conferences. It was agreed that the program and its purposes should be discussed with member banks. A second method of encouraging use of reserves was establishment of district committees. In May, 1932, the Federal Reserve Bank of New York appointed a committee of district bankers and businessmen to help develop ways and means of making effective use of funds made available by the program of open market purchases. The Board of Governors approved of the committee and suggested that similar committees be established in the other Reserve Districts.

After July, the System's portfolio of Government securities remained at about the same level for the rest of the year even though there was no change in the policy of more active ease. A return flow of currency and gold imports resulted in a substantial rise in excess reserves.

The effects of the open market program was a subject of frequent discussion, especially since its desirability was a subject of controversy. Some, especially those who had consistently opposed substantial purchases from the beginning of the depression, did not think they were effective in promoting recovery. As excess reserves began to build up, failure of member banks to put the reserves to use became an influential argument against additional purchases. Others thought the effects were confined to the large financial centers.

But the advocates of a more active program pointed to several beneficial effects. Even though the securities were purchased in New York and the initial impact was on reserves of New York City banks, the easing effects were much more widespread. Treasury operations and ordinary business transactions shifted these funds to banks and other institutions throughout the country. The funds supplied by purchases resulted in easier conditions in the money market and lower market rates. Another beneficial effect of the purchase program was a reduction in member-bank indebtedness and assistance in meeting the reserve drain resulting from currency withdrawal and at times gold exports.

COOPERATING WITH THE RECOVERY PROGRAM

At a joint meeting of the Board of Governors and the Open Market Policy Conference early in January, 1933, the situation was carefully reviewed, and it was decided that the policy of maintaining substantial excess reserves should be continued. With member-bank indebtedness at a low level and the forces of deflation having subsided in the latter part of 1932, officials thought open market policy could be less concerned with immediate objectives such as contributing to safety in enabling banks to meet deposit withdrawals and in dealing with the forces of deflation. A statement adopted at the joint meeting indicated the shift in emphasis: "The larger objectives of the System's open market policy, to assist and accelerate the forces of recovery, are now assuming importance."

But what appeared to be a trend toward recovery was soon to be interrupted by a deepening financial crisis and a bank holiday in early March. Following the bank holiday and a comprehensive review of System policy, there was general agreement that the Federal Reserve should cooperate in every way possible to help carry out the Government's national recovery program. There was a consensus that with excess reserves still substantial, it was not desirable to buy Government securities to increase bank reserves.

The Open Market Policy Conference, however, agreed that the Executive Committee should be given authority to make such purchases as might be necessary to assist the Treasury in its financing. There was apprehension that if the Treasury could not do its financing successfully in the market, it would be forced to seek accommodation directly from the Reserve Banks. The Conference recommended that the Executive Committee be authorized to purchase up to $1 billion of Governments, if necessary, to make it possible for the Treasury to meet its requirements. The Executive Committee was also given authority to shift maturities

—engage in swap transactions—in order to promote a better rate relationship among maturities and to tone up the market for Treasury issues.

The Board of Governors approved the recommendation of the Conference but without the limitation that purchases were to be for the purpose of assisting the Treasury. The Board thought it might be desirable to make purchases for other purposes. In fact, one Board member favored an "energetic" program of purchases on the basis that substantial purchases immediately would be more effective than the same amount spread over a longer period.

Substantial purchases of Government securities were made and excess reserves rose rapidly during the summer. By early fall, excess reserves were so large that most officials thought there was no need for further purchases to supply reserves or ease credit; however, it was agreed that purchases should continue for a while, primarily to reflect continued cooperation with the national recovery program.

In October, there was a full-scale review of policy. Excess reserves were about $760 million, member-bank indebtedness to the Reserve Banks was at the lowest level since August, 1917, and short-term interest rates were at an all-time low. There was general agreement that additional purchases were not needed for monetary reasons. Instead, the problem was primarily one of achieving more effective use of reserves and funds already supplied.

A resolution adopted by the Open Market Committee, following extended discussion, pointed out that open market operations had not yet achieved the intended objectives and the reasons why:

Open market operations, as a means of stimulating business recovery, are ordinarily designed to force banking funds, first, into the short-time money market, and subsequently, as short-time rates are lowered, into the intermediate- and long-time capital markets. In the present instance, it seems clear that neither of these major purposes is yet accomplished.[7]

The resolution pointed out that there were grave obstacles to the use of both short- and longer-term credit. Failure of short-

---

[7] Memorandum entitled "Memorandum of Open Market Policy," submitted to the Federal Open Market Committee at its meeting of October 10, 1933.

term credit to expand reflected unwillingness on the part of both borrowers and lenders. Business firms were unwilling to borrow because they had had several years of unprofitable operations and had suffered a huge shrinkage in value of assets. Banks, after having been subjected to waves of deposit withdrawals and failures for several years, were pursuing a policy of extreme liquidity. The flow of credit into intermediate- and longer-term uses was blocked by lack of confidence. The capital issue market was completely stagnant and the capital goods industries were responsible for over 60 per cent of the unemployment.

The conclusion was:

> *In our judgement, these conditions indicate that the effectiveness of open market operations, in so far as banking and credit factors are concerned, will depend in large measure upon the early adoption of a broader program, designed to strengthen confidence and to encourage the flow of credit, both short-time and long-time, into uses which make for a well-balanced and enduring recovery.*[8]

The policy of buying Government securities to build up and maintain excess reserves ended in the latter part of 1933. There was little need for purchases in the remainder of the decade as gold imports pushed excess reserves to higher and higher levels. In reviewing open market operations for the period 1930–1933, the Board concluded:

> *. . . the placing of reserve funds in the market through the purchase of United States Government securities has been an effective means of preventing exceptional demands upon the member banks from tightening the credit situation and that these funds have been a powerful means toward the establishment and maintenance of ease in the short-term money market. Although the abundant credit provided was not effectively employed by business, it would appear that the maintenance continuously of a substantial volume of excess reserves through open-market purchases helped to arrest a powerful deflationary movement and created conditions propitious to business recovery.*[9]

---

[8] Minutes, Federal Open Market Committee, October 12, 1933.
[9] Annual Report of the Federal Reserve Board, 1933, p. 21.

6. A NEW PROBLEM: EXCESS RESERVES

. . . the special problem created by the continuing excess of reserves has had and will continue to have the unremitting study and attention of those charged with the responsibility for credit policy in order that appropriate action may be taken as soon as it appears to be in the public interest.

—*Annual Report of the Board of Governors, 1935*

The Federal Reserve's position with respect to credit and the money market was fundamentally altered during the remainder of the decade. Before the end of 1933, excess reserves of member banks reached $800 million. Large gold imports following devaluation of the dollar pushed excess reserves above $3 billion late in 1935. By the end of the decade excess reserves were above $5 billion even though reserve requirements were close to the maximum authorized under the law. Excess reserves in relation to required reserves in the mid-thirties were equivalent to about $21 billion excess reserves early in 1965; at the end of the decade they were the equivalent of nearly $16 billion.

Excess reserves were so large that the System could not exert real restraint, should the need arise. The discount rate was ineffective because member banks rarely needed to borrow. Open market operations were ineffective because System holdings of securities ranged around $2.5 billion during most of the period from 1933 to the end of 1939.

APPRAISAL OF THE SITUATION

There was extended discussion of the business and credit situation in the latter part of 1935. The consensus of the Board of Governors and Open Market Committee was that business and

75

financial conditions were continuing to improve but the economy was still far short of full recovery. There was no evidence of over-expansion in use of credit or in business activity. Gold imports had pushed member-bank reserves far beyond present or prospec-tive credit requirements for sound business expansion. In this situation, the primary objective of Federal Reserve policy "is still to lend its efforts to a furtherance of recovery."

Federal Reserve officials were apprehensive, however, about several aspects of the economic situation and their implications for the future. Their concern centered around three main points.

First, as long as the channels into private capital investment remained blocked and the Government debt continued to expand there was grave danger that excess reserves would result in an increase in bank holdings of Government securities and the desired spill-over of funds into private channels might not occur. As a result, commercial banks might become more and more heavily loaded with Government securities.

Second, should excess reserves continue to flow primarily into commercial bank investment in Governments, experience in other countries indicated that eventually a point is reached when banks are unable or unwilling to absorb more Government securities. In that event, the Government would be forced to request the Reserve Banks to buy Government securities in the market, borrow directly from the Reserve Banks, or issue some form of inconvertible paper money. Financing a Government deficit through the banking system or through the issue of paper money, if long continued, usually led eventually to rapidly rising prices and inflation.

Third, the situation differed from Government deficit financing which had usually led to uncontrollable inflation, in that the Government's extraordinary expenditures were the result of de-pression. In depression, in contrast to a boom, some expansion of credit is essential and it is the duty of the central bank to facilitate it.

Officials were disturbed as to the significance of these develop-ments because past experience or accepted theory of central banking provided no guidance as to their implications for future policy. Before the war, the generally accepted rule of central banking had been that the discount rate should be increased when there was an outflow of gold; yet when the Federal Reserve applied this rule in the fall of 1931, some thought the rate increase probably served more to add to the deflationary movement than to check the outflow of gold.

Neither theory nor experience was a useful guide as to proper policy when there were substantial excess reserves. Large excess reserves and a steadily mounting Government debt could sooner or later lead to inflation, but there was not sufficient evidence of these developments to justify a reduction in holdings of Government securities and reversal of the policy of monetary ease. Officials believed that for open market policy to be successful it should be part of an over-all program, including removal of obstacles and restoring confidence, to promote the flow of funds into the private capital market, and to increase availability and lower the cost of mortgage money.

Large excess reserves and unusually low short-term market rates, led some officials to suggest liquidating some of the System's holdings of Government securities.[1] In fact, in the spring of 1935, one Reserve Bank requested permission to reduce its portfolio of Governments. Most officials, however, were opposed. They thought low market rates reflected not only the large supply of excess reserves, but small demand for credit and preference of banks and other lenders for open market investments instead of loans. There was no reason for any action to raise rates so long as there was no prospect of an excessive use of funds by borrowers. There was a large volume of excess reserves, but no evidence of *excessive use* of bank credit. Another advantage of retaining Government securities holdings was to have a portfolio available as an instrument of restraint should an inflationary situation develop.

EXCESS RESERVES: A DILEMMA

The large and growing volume of excess reserves was rapidly depriving the System of its capability to regulate credit and the money supply. The economy, still short of full recovery, called for

---

[1] Dealers' quotations on three-month U.S. Treasury bills in 1935 ranged from 0.15 to 0.20 per cent.

continuation of the easy money policy. The dilemma: how absorb or immobilize enough excess reserves to restore System control over credit without adverse effects on business recovery.❚ ❚There was unanimous agreement that the System should continue to pursue an easy money policy. Widespread increases in business activity indicated real progress toward recovery, but there was still large-scale unemployment, little private investment, and total output was substantially below the pre-depression level.❚

On the other hand, there was increasing concern over the System's inability to restrict credit expansion should the need arise sometime in the future. The discount rate was ineffective because member banks rarely needed to borrow from the Reserve Banks. By the end of 1935, excess reserves were much larger than the System's portfolio of Government securities; hence liquidation of the entire portfolio would not put the System in a position to exercise effective restraint. Maximum use of the new authority to raise reserve requirements would leave a substantial margin of excess reserves. There was general agreement that excess reserves should be reduced, but the crucial question was whether it could be done without jeopardizing business recovery.

System officials devoted much thought and discussion to the unusual situation—partial business recovery, huge excess reserves, and potential dangers inherent in its position of impotence. The Federal Open Market Committee at a three-day meeting in the latter part of October, 1935, adopted unanimously a resolution summarizing its views. The more pertinent parts are given below:

> *The Committee reviewed the preliminary memorandum submitted by the Chairman and discussed at length business and credit conditions and the banking position in relation to them. It was the unanimous opinion of the Committee that the primary objective of the System at the present time is still to lend its efforts towards the furtherance of recovery. While much progress has been made, it cannot be said that business activity on the whole is yet normal, or that the effects of the depression are yet overcome. Statistics of business activity and business credit activity, both short and long term, do not show any undue expansion. In these circumstances, the Committee was unanimously of the opinion that there is nothing in the business or credit situation which at this time necessitates the adoption of any policy designed to retard credit expansion.*

But the Committee cannot fail to recognize that the rapid growth of bank deposits and bank reserves in the past year and a half is building up a credit base which may be very difficult to control if undue credit expansion should become evident. The continued large imports of gold and silver serve to increase the magnitude of that problem. Even now actual reserves of member banks are more than double their requirements, and there is no evidence of a let-up in their growth. That being so, the Committee is of the opinion that steps should be taken by the Reserve System as promptly as may be possible to absorb at least some of these excess reserves, not with a view to checking some further expansion of credit, but rather to put the System in a better position to act effectively in the event that credit expansion should go too far.

Two methods of absorbing excess reserves have been discussed by the Committee: (a) the sale of short-term Government securities by the Federal Reserve System, and (b) the raising of reserve requirements.[2]

Selling Government securities to absorb excess reserves involved two significant risks. Sales might be a shock to the bond market and induce a wave of selling by banks. A second hazard was that even though accompanied by a public explanation, sales of securities might be construed by the public as a major reversal of credit policy because up to that time sales had been used as a means of restraint. A majority of the Committee opposed sales of Government securities because of the risks involved.

Raising reserve requirements also involved risks. This was a new and untried tool, and higher requirements might restrain desirable expansion of credit. Before employing this method, the Committee suggested that the Board of Governors make a thorough study of the amount and location of excess reserves by districts and class of bank to determine the extent to which an increase in reserve requirements might interfere with loan and investment expansion by member banks. The Committee recognized that in making suggestions regarding reserve requirements it was going beyond its own immediate jurisdiction, but thought open market policy could not be determined independently of other Federal Reserve policies.[3]

The Board made a study to determine the impact of a possible increase in reserve requirements on the reserve position of individual member banks. Using call-report data for November 1,

---

[2] Annual Report of the Board of Governors, 1935, pp. 231–232.

[3] It should be noted that the Board of Governors constituted a majority of the 12-member Open Market Committee as reorganized by the Banking Act of 1935.

1935, they found that 47 per cent of country member banks, 33 per cent of central reserve city members, and 30 per cent of reserve city banks had excess reserves of 100 per cent and over of required reserves. Member banks with excess reserves of less than 25 per cent of required reserves accounted for only 19 per cent of country members and about 35 per cent of central reserve and reserve city banks. Only 112 member banks had insufficient excess reserves and correspondent balances combined, to meet a 50 per cent increase in reserve requirements.

Reserve requirements was the method favored to absorb excess reserves and the Board of Governors raised requirements by steps, from August, 1936 to May, 1937, to the maximum permitted under the law.[4]

At its meeting on January 30, 1937, when the final increases were decided upon, the Board prepared a press statement for release the following day, explaining that the increases were not intended as a move away from an easy money policy. The purpose was to reestablish System control over reserves and the money supply. The principal reasons for raising reserve requirements are covered in the following excerpts from the statement:

> *The Board estimates that, after the full increase has gone into effect, member banks will have excess reserves of approximately $500,000,000, an amount ample to finance further recovery and to maintain easy money conditions. At the same time the Federal Reserve System will be placed in a position where such reduction or expansion of member bank reserves as may be deemed in the public interest may be effected through open-market operations, a more flexible instrument, better adapted for keeping the reserve position of member banks currently in close adjustment to credit needs. . . .*
>
> *The present is an opportune time for action because . . . excess reserves are widely distributed among member banks, and balances with correspondent banks are twice as large as they have generally been in the past. . . .*
>
> *Another reason for action at this time is that . . . 'it is far better to sterilize a part of these superfluous reserves while they are still unused than to permit a credit structure to be erected upon them and then to withdraw the foundation of the structure.'*[5]

---

[4] Effective in late December, 1936, the Treasury also initiated a new policy of sterilizing the effect of gold imports on bank reserves. The increase in member bank reserves arising from payment for the gold by Treasury check on a Reserve Bank was offset by the Treasury withdrawing the funds from its tax and loan deposits or from the market. Previously, the Treasury had issued an equivalent amount of gold certificates to the Reserve Banks to restore its deposit in the Reserve Banks which had been drawn down by payment for the gold.

[5] Annual Report of the Board of Governors, 1937, pp. 196–197.

The Federal Open Market Committee undertook to stabilize the Government securities market in the spring of 1937—increases in reserve requirements were effective in March and May—in order to facilitate member-bank adjustments needed in meeting the higher requirements. A small number of banks increased their sales of Government securities, principally long-term bonds on which they had profits instead of short-term issues. As long-term rates began to rise, the System bought long-term Governments to help stabilize the market. Purchases of bonds in March and April totaled about $200 million, the reserve effect being partially offset by a reduction in holdings of short-term issues. The yield on long-term Governments rose from about 2½ to about 2¾ per cent in early April and then began to decline. Excess reserves, after the final increase in reserve requirements became effective May 1, were about $900 million.

Whether System officials were temporarily successful in achieving their twin goals of absorbing excess reserves to restore some measure of System control but without adverse effects on business is, at least for some people, debatable. The System was in a better position to exercise some control over bank reserve positions because excess reserves, although still large, were reduced to less than one-half of Federal Reserve holdings of Government securities. But the effects on business have been a subject of controversy. Some critics have alleged that the increase in reserve requirements was an important cause of the recession which began in mid-1937.[6]

The increase in reserve requirements brought excess reserves within the boundary of Federal Reserve control for only a short time. Gold imports continued and had pushed excess reserves above System holdings of Government securities by mid-1938. By the end of 1940, excess reserves had soared to almost $7 billion, and the Board of Governors, presidents of the Reserve

---

[6] Available data suggest that adverse effects, if any, were largely of psychological origin. For example, after the final increase in reserve requirements had become effective in May, 1937, just prior to the onset of the depression, excess reserves were over $900 million (equivalent in terms of required reserves to over $3 billion excess reserves in January, 1965); member-bank borrowing from Reserve Banks, monthly average, was $16 million; the discount rate of the Federal Reserve Bank of New York was 1½ per cent; dealers' quotations on three-month U.S. Treasury bills averaged 0.41 per cent and market yields on three- to five-year U.S. Treasury notes (tax exempt) averaged 1.48 per cent; the call-loan rate was 1 per cent; and the market rate on four- to six-month prime commercial paper averaged 1 per cent.

Banks, and Federal Advisory Council joined in submitting a report to the Congress. The report pointed out that the System's powers were inadequate to cope with the problem of excess reserves. The principal recommendations may be summarized as follows:

1. Congress should provide means for absorbing a large part of existing excess reserves (about $7 billion) as well as additions that may occur. Specific proposals that might be considered were: raising the legal maxima for reserve requirements; giving the Federal Open Market Committee power to make further increases in reserve requirements sufficient to absorb excess reserves provided the requirements should not be raised to more than double the recommended statutory maxima and empowering the Committee to change reserve requirements for any or all classifications of member banks; and making the proposed reserve requirements applicable to all commercial banks.

2. Sources of potential increases in excess reserves, such as authority under the Thomas inflation amendment to issue $3 billion of greenbacks, further monetization of foreign silver, and the power to issue silver certificates, should be removed.

3. Means should be found to prevent further growth in excess reserves and in deposits arising from future gold acquisitions. Gold imports should be insulated from the credit system and should not be restored to it except after consultation with the Open Market Committee.

4. Financing both the ordinary expenditures of the Government and the defense program should be from existing deposits rather than by creating deposits through bank purchases of Government securities.

5. As national income increases, a larger and larger portion of defense expenses should be met out of taxes rather than by borrowing; and once the country approaches full utilization of its economic capacity, the budget should be balanced.

A NEW OBJECTIVE EMERGES

The large volume of excess reserves and continued economic stagnation altered official thinking about use of the tools. The discount rate would not be effective so long as member banks did not need to borrow. Open market operations were not very effective either, as we have seen, under conditions prevailing in the late thirties. There was no need for purchases to supply reserves, and sales were not regarded as a suitable method of absorbing excess reserves because of the danger of an unfavorable impact on the money and capital markets and hence on economic recovery. Furthermore, the System's portfolio was too small to absorb a major part of excess reserves. Open market operations had been rendered almost completely ineffective as a tool for altering bank reserve positions and thereby influencing bank credit and the money supply.

With excess reserves having rendered normal use of the System's tools ineffective, the question arose as to what could be done to influence the economy. As a result of the unusual combination of circumstances in the latter part of the thirties, open market operations gradually came to be used for a new intermediate objective—to help stabilize the Government securities market instead of to alter reserve positions.

In December, 1934, the Open Market Committee had authorized the Executive Committee to make swaps among maturities in the System's portfolio, up to a total of $100 million, if desirable in helping maintain stability in the Government securities market or in connection with Treasury financing operations. At the same time, a member of the Committee raised questions as to whether open market operations should be confined to short-term Government securities, whether further shifts from short- to long-term securities should be made at appropriate times, and whether the System should be prepared to support the Government securities market "vigorously and independently" without waiting for requests from the Treasury.

The role of the Federal Reserve System in the Government securities market became a topic of frequent discussion. Early in 1935, Treasury officials, concerned over the extremely rapid rise in Government bond prices, inquired whether the System could exert some restraining influence on excessively rapid price fluctuations in order that the market would be in a sound condition for the Treasury's March financing. Treasury officials contended this was more logically the responsibility of the Federal Reserve than the Treasury because it involved regulation of the money market. Some Federal Reserve officials, however, were concerned as to public reaction should a policy of cushioning Government securities price movements require sales from the System's portfolio. The state of the Government securities market had become significant because it was the dominant factor in the money market. System officials agreed that it was not desirable to peg Government securities prices at any point, but that it might be desirable in certain conditions to cushion movements in either direction. The System bought some long-term bonds in the spring of 1935, in order to help maintain an orderly market.

When reserve requirements were increased in the spring of 1937, the Federal Open Market Committee authorized shifts in the System's portfolio "with a view to preventing a disorderly market." In April, 1937, the Executive Committee was directed to make such purchases and sales as may be necessary "to preserving an orderly market." In April, 1938, to avoid a too rapid or too extensive rise in bond prices, the Executive Committee was again authorized to conduct open market operations for the purpose of maintaining orderly market conditions.

The huge volume of excess reserves led System officials to the conclusion that they had a better chance of exercising a stabilizing influence on the economy by using open market operations to maintain a stable Government securities market instead of to influence bank reserves. Government securities had become the dominant segment of the securities market, and banks had acquired substantial holdings of Governments. Maintaining an orderly Government securities market tended to stabilize the capital market and banking, thus facilitating the flow of credit into business and investment uses.

This shift in the intermediate objective of open market operations resulted in a change in composition of the System's portfolio of Government securities. Short-term securities were considered better suited to prompt and possibly large sales or purchases to absorb or supply reserves. But a better distribution of maturities was needed when the objective was maintaining orderly conditions in the Government securities market. Reflecting this shift in emphasis, the System began, in 1939, to increase substantially its holdings of longer-term Governments.

7. WORLD WAR II: PEGGED RATES

Another joint aim of the Treasury and the Federal Reserve
was to maintain prices and yields on Government securities close
to existing levels for the duration of the war.

—Annual Report of the Board of Governors, 1942

As war clouds gathered in Europe in the late thirties, the authorities began to consider what the System's role should be in assisting the Treasury finance a stepped-up defense program. A special meeting of the Conference of Presidents was called in September, 1938, to consider policies and programs the System might adopt in the event of an outbreak of war in Europe. The consensus was that the Federal Reserve should maintain a reasonable measure of liquidity in the Government securities market and announce a uniform policy of lending to member banks on the par value of Government securities offered as collateral. There was a series of meetings between Federal Reserve and Treasury representatives in the first part of 1939 to consider mutual problems and policies in case of war. There was agreement that in the event of war, steps should be taken to stabilize the Government securities market.

A question which arose was whether the System and the Treasury should participate in stabilization of the Government securities market. It was agreed that the System would participate equally with the Treasury in purchases of Government securities until the Treasury had invested approximately $100 million available from trust funds. Thereafter all purchases should be made by the System. The System's reasoning was that after purchases of approximately $100 million the Treasury would have to draw on the stabilization fund. The result would be, in effect, to create an open market portfolio in the Treasury

85

that might interfere with the System's ability to control credit. The System had adequate authority to purchase Government securities to stabilize the market and the consensus was that it should assume that responsibility.

How open market operations could be used to stabilize a seriously disturbed market was also discussed. The conclusion was that the System should make purchases at scaled-down prices until certain agreed minimum prices for the day had been reached, then with the cooperation of the principal dealers in Government securities, trading would be stopped as far as possible for the day. On subsequent trading days, purchases would be resumed at the minimum prices of the preceding day and the same procedure followed. The Open Market Committee thought it should be made clear that short selling during any period of disturbed conditions would be strongly objected to.

Following the outbreak of war in Europe, System responsibility to assist the Treasury in financing the defense effort was given more extensive consideration. Early in 1941, the Open Market Committee instructed the Executive Committee to have studies prepared on the System's role in Treasury financing operations. Memoranda were prepared and circulated among officials, and the System's role in war financing became a major topic of discussion at policy conferences.

Four alternatives regarding System policy in war financing were presented to the Open Market Committee for consideration and discussion in the fall of 1941: allow market rates to fluctuate freely in response to changing supply and demand; try to maintain an orderly market for Government securities; if new powers were granted,[1] tighten credit and let interest rates rise; or establish a pattern of rates, to be agreed on from time to time with Treasury officials, which the System would support. There seemed to be considerable sentiment for establishing a pattern of rates in order to avoid one of the difficulties of World War I financing, namely, rising rates which afforded an inducement for investors to defer purchases of new Treasury issues. But it was

---

[1] As explained in Chapter 6, pp. 81–82, excess reserves were so large that the System submitted a special report to Congress explaining the nature of the problem and making certain proposals regarding new powers to deal with it.

recognized that this alternative involved the problem of whether the System could maintain a pattern of rates and at the same time effectively combat inflation.

WAR FINANCING

The day after the Japanese attack on Pearl Harbor the Board of Governors, after consultation with the presidents of the Federal Reserve Banks, made it clear that as in World War I the primary objective of Federal Reserve policy would be to facilitate financing the war. The statement issued included the following:

> *The System is prepared to use its powers to assure that an ample supply of funds is available at all times for financing the war effort and to exert its influence toward maintaining conditions in the United States Government security market that are satisfactory from the standpoint of the Government's requirements.*[2]

The principal question was how this objective could best be achieved.

Role of the central bank

System officials agreed that in time of war the primary responsibility of a central bank was to facilitate financing the expenditures involved in national defense. The primary goal of Federal Reserve policy was to assure that funds needed in financing the war would be forthcoming. Preventing inflation, although desirable, was secondary.

System policymakers believed the Federal Reserve had a subordinate role in an over-all program designed to finance the war without inflation. The major problem was to divert income as well as productive facilities to the war effort.[3] For example, the Chairman of the Board of Governors, referring to the fact that

---

[2] Annual Report of the Board of Governors, 1941, p. 1.

[3] The Board of Governors, by Executive Order of the President of the United States, was directed to control consumer credit during the national emergency. The Board issued Regulation W, effective September 1, 1941, prescribing minimum down payments and limitations on maturities. The main purposes of the regulation were to curtail demand for selected consumer durables as diversion of productive resources to national defense limited their supply, and to restrict general expansion of consumer credit.

national income was about $110 billion, stated that "upwards of 50 billions of civilian dollars must be drawn into the war effort and not left to compete in the market place for the shrinking supply of civilian goods. Otherwise, the rising tide of national income would rapidly bid up prices and precipitate a ruinous inflation." To the extent that the required amount of income was not diverted to war financing by taxation, it should be diverted by Government borrowing out of current income. Borrowing from the banking system would create more money without adding to the supply of goods. Federal Reserve credit control, although important, had only a supplementary role to Government policies in preventing inflation.

Pattern of rates

The anchor of System policy to facilitate Treasury financing was establishment and maintenance of a pattern of rates on Government securities. A pegged rate structure, it was believed, would assure the Treasury of a market for its securities and would remove any incentive for investors to defer purchases in order to get a higher rate.

Discussion of interest rates that would be appropriate in the event of war began in the late thirties, as already mentioned. In mid-1941, one Federal Reserve official suggested that a $2\frac{1}{2}$ per cent rate on long-term Government securities should be established for the duration of the emergency. The feasibility of establishing a pattern of rates for different maturities of Government securities was seriously discussed in the latter part of 1941 and explored in joint meetings of System and Treasury officials.

System officials did not want to make a commitment to support a given pattern of rates regardless of the type of financing program the Treasury might pursue. They wanted such a commitment to be contingent on the Treasury adopting a borrowing program designed to attract as much nonbank funds as possible. Early in 1942, the System submitted to Treasury officials a suggested long-term program of Treasury financing, which had the general approval of the Open Market Committee, including the presidents who were not official members.

The major points in the program were:

1. The Treasury should issue securities tailored to meet the requirements of different classes of investors in order to attract the maximum amount of nonbank funds. Special issues should be on tap in order to keep Treasury financing in the open market and sale of Treasury securities to banks to a minimum.

2. If open market financing were kept to a minimum the Federal Reserve would do everything in its power to assure the success of such financing.

3. The Treasury should undertake to finance the war at a rate not to exceed $2\frac{1}{2}$ per cent; in the event of a public statement by the Treasury, no reference should be made as to maturity of long-term bonds in order to provide more flexibility.

4. The point at which support would be given to the market by the Federal Reserve would be determined in discussions with the Treasury from time to time. .

5. The System preferred that rates on shorter maturities remain flexible in order better to adapt to changing conditions.

Treasury officials were reluctant to agree to a long-term program of financing, preferring to make decisions as each financing arose. System authorities, although cognizant that it would not be feasible to decide on detailed terms of all future issues, were anxious to have an agreement on certain basic principles that would be followed. For one thing, they wanted agreement on establishing a $2\frac{1}{2}$ per cent long-term rate for the duration as a benchmark, rates on other maturities being fixed according to existing market rates.

An agreement was reached with Treasury representatives in March, 1942, with respect to a temporary program of war financing. Federal Reserve authorities agreed to support the Treasury bill market at approximately existing rates, support beginning when the rate reached $\frac{1}{4}$ of 1 per cent and then to be applied with increasing strength as the rate approached $\frac{3}{8}$ of 1 per cent.[4] The general market would be maintained on about the existing curve of rates but this did not mean support for specific issues that might be out of line with the yield curve.

---

[4] For an explanation of the divergent views of Federal Reserve and Treasury authorities over short-term rates and the volume of excess reserves, see Chapter 11, pp. 145–148.

Open market policy was directed at two major wartime objectives: maintaining the existing structure of rates on Government securities, and maintaining an adequate supply of reserves to facilitate Treasury financing. This twofold objective was reflected in the Open Market Committee's directive to the Executive Committee in May, 1942, to conduct such transactions "as may be necessary for the purpose of maintaining about the present general level of prices and yields of Government securities or for the purpose of maintaining an adequate supply of funds in the market; . . . ."

Disagreement over the volume of excess reserves that should be maintained, explained in more detail later, led to a compromise regarding short-term rates. Briefly, the Treasury's position was that a large volume of excess reserves was essential in order to maintain the rate pattern and assure the success of its borrowing operations. The System's position was that large excess reserves were neither necessary nor desirable so long as open market operations were used to maintain the rate pattern. Open market operations required to maintain the rate structure would automatically provide the amount of reserves needed.

System officials, even though they preferred somewhat higher short-term rates, agreed to establish a posted buying rate of $\frac{3}{8}$ per cent on U. S. Treasury bills. The posted buying rate was established to increase the fluidity of bank reserves and facilitate prompt adjustment of bank reserve positions; to encourage banks and other institutions to invest liquid funds in Treasury bills; and to stabilize the bill market. Later in the year, the System added a repurchase option—the seller being given the option of repurchasing Treasury bills of like amount and maturity at the same rate of discount. The repurchase option was designed to encourage investment of idle funds and a wider distribution of Treasury bills. The practical effect was to make bank holdings of Treasury bills the equivalent of reserves.

Other System policies

The discount rate was lowered to 1 per cent, and loans to member banks collateralled by Government securities maturing within one year were given a preferential rate of $\frac{1}{2}$ per cent. Low discount rates and a preferential rate on Governments were additional methods of assuring member banks of ready access to reserves in order that they might better perform the functions of purchaser and distributer of Treasury securities.

Federal Reserve authorities tried to discourage nonessential uses of credit in order to help hold down total credit expansion and the pressure on limited productive resources. As already stated, the purpose of Regulation W was to curtail use of credit to purchase civilian goods in short supply. Selective controls, such as consumer credit and margin requirements on stock market credit, differed from general controls, according to System officials, in two major respects. First, they limit the amount of credit users can demand for specified purposes; they are selective in their impact. Second, they do not affect the total volume and cost of credit inasmuch as credit not used for regulated purposes may be made available for nonregulated purposes.

Federal Reserve officials, in cooperation with other bank supervisory authorities, instructed bank examiners to urge bankers to be selective in making loans; to curtail loans for accumulation of inventories of civilian goods and other nonproductive purposes. They also warned of the dangers inherent in making loans to buy real estate at rising prices.

Problems with pattern of rates

Maintaining the pattern of rates became increasingly difficult. As some Federal Reserve officials pointed out, a policy of maintaining substantial excess reserves, a fixed pattern of rates, and urging banks to keep fully invested was inconsistent and contradictory. Easy access to reserves encouraged banks to keep fully invested. But to the extent banks kept fully invested, it was impossible to keep a large volume of excess reserves outstanding.

As investors gained confidence in the Federal Reserve's willingness and ability to maintain the rate pattern there was a growing tendency to "play the pattern of rates." With all maturities almost equally liquid, there was a strong inducement to sell lower-yield, short-term securities and reinvest in higher-yield, longer maturities. To maintain the pattern of rates, the Federal

Reserve was compelled to buy short-term Governments which investors were unwilling to hold. The question facing the Federal Reserve was whether to make a strong effort to maintain a pattern of rates established in a period of economic stagnation when the volume of excess reserves and other idle funds was unusually large, when the demand for credit was limited, and when preference for liquidity was high; or whether the pattern should be modified to provide a rate structure that would be easier to support.

Several suggestions to help alleviate the situation were discussed. System officials continued to press for an upward adjustment in short-term rates in order to narrow the spread between short- and long-term yields. A narrower spread would offer less inducement for playing the pattern of rates and tend to reduce the volume of reserves created by System purchases of Treasury bills and other short-term issues. Treasury officials were opposed to higher short-term rates. They did not want to disturb a market which had enabled the Treasury to do its financing so successfully.

Another proposal, by a System official, was to purchase bills directly from the Treasury to supply reserves in periods of Treasury financing. He thought direct purchases would enable the System to bypass the market and better gear reserves supplied to the amount needed to facilitate a Treasury offering. But others pointed out some disadvantages. Direct purchases might arouse public concern about the Government's credit standing; and it was doubted whether direct purchases from the Treasury would make possible a better synchronizing of reserves supplied with reserves needed to facilitate a Treasury financing operation.

As an alternative to raising short-term rates outright, it was suggested that the Treasury might issue a ¾ per cent, nine-month certificate which the System would stand ready to buy under a repurchase option. The policy of maintaining rates on maturities of less than nine months would then be terminated. But this proposal also had serious disadvantages. Some officials thought a new type of security would upset the market. More important, it would not solve the problem of playing the pattern of rates because investors were already moving into longer maturities which afforded larger profit opportunities.

As implications of the support policy became more widely recognized and as confidence increased that the rate pattern would be maintained, investor demand was concentrated in higher-yielding, long-term issues. The result was to exert strong pressure toward a level rate structure because under the support policy all maturities were liquid. The policy of keeping banks supplied with ample reserves in order that they could be the market of last resort for Government securities intensified the pressure.

MORE RESEARCH

Marked changes in business, and in banking and credit accompanied the war. The need for more information on current and prospective changes in the economy led to an expanded and better coordinated research program.

Early in the war the Conference of Presidents established a standing committee on research to help coordinate the research programs of the Reserve Banks, assist in bringing about closer cooperation between the research staffs of the Reserve Banks and the Board of Governors, and to help promote a more effective use of research facilities within the System. The presidents also believed that the growing importance of the role of Reserve Banks as regional centers of information and leadership made it advisable to develop the Banks' research facilities. In view of varying regional impacts of the war, regional studies were needed to keep informed on district developments and to provide a better basis for national policies.

Additional steps were taken in 1944 to coordinate research activities of the System. The System Research Advisory Committee was established to guide and coordinate the research work of the Board and the Reserve Banks. Another System committee was established to study the current and prospective position of banking in view of policies being pursued in financing the war, and to anticipate possible postwar problems and policies for dealing with them. System research staffs were also cooperating with other agencies at the national and district levels.

8. SQUIRMING IN A STRAITJACKET

The creation of unnecessary bank credit by the commercial banking system is the particular concern of those charged with monetary responsibilities. It can not be a matter of indifference that at present the country's central banking mechanism lacks appropriate means, that may be needed, to restrain unnecessary creation of bank credit through continued acquisition of Government or other securities by the commercial banks.

—Annual Report of the Board of Governors, 1945

System officials, as already noted, had been trying to anticipate postwar problems long before World War II was over. Studies were initiated to provide more information on changing business and credit conditions; the impact of Federal Reserve-Treasury wartime policies, nationally and regionally; and the implication of these changes for monetary policy.

Important questions confronting policymakers at the end of the war were: What should be the objective of open market policy in the postwar environment; should the System continue to maintain a pattern of rates on Government securities; if so, would this seriously interfere with effective regulation of credit and the money supply; and, in the event of conflict, which objective should take priority?

IMPLICATIONS OF NEW ENVIRONMENT

Despite general agreement that war expenditures should be financed as far as possible by taxation, about 60 per cent of total Government expenditures came from borrowing. From June 30, 1940, about the beginning of the defense program, to the end of 1945, the Government raised $228 billion by borrowing. Of this

94

total, $95 billion, or 40 per cent, was derived from selling Government securities to the commercial banking system. The money supply—demand deposits plus currency in circulation—increased more than threefold, from $40 billion to $127 billion. In addition, highly liquid assets held by the general public soared. Time deposits nearly doubled, and Government securities held by the public (excluding banks and other financial institutions) were about eight times larger than in mid-1940.

Inflation potential

• There was general expectation that military demobilization and reconversion from war to civilian production would result in substantial unemployment and recession. These fears did not materialize, however, one reason being the substantial volume of money and liquid assets at the disposal of the public.

Federal Reserve officials were aware of the large inflation potential created in financing the war. The public had at its disposal large resources in money and other liquid assets. Current income was at a high level. Wartime controls, and to some extent depressed conditions in the thirties, had built up a huge backlog of demand for civilian goods. The combination of pent-up demand supported by a high level of income and accumulated purchasing power was likely to unleash a tremendous flow of funds into the market for civilian goods. The country's money supply and purchasing power were—and would likely continue to be for an indefinite period—far in excess of the supply of goods available for money to buy at stable prices.

To deal effectively with this inflationary situation called for a broad approach directed at the basic sources of inflationary pressure. Of first importance, according to System officials, was to relieve the shortage of goods by rapid attainment of full production. The Government's excess cash balance should be used to retire outstanding debt, especially securities held by commercial banks, because it would tend to reduce the money supply. Vigorous efforts should be made to achieve a budget surplus in order that debt reduction might continue. Preventing excessive expansion of bank credit and creation of new money, the particular responsibility of the Federal Reserve System, was regarded as only one part of an over-all program needed to combat the inflation potential existing at the end of the war.

Dilemma of the Federal Reserve

The Federal Reserve faced essentially the same dilemma as at the end of World War I. System officials could maintain the unusually low wartime rate structure which would facilitate the Treasury's large financing operations but in a postwar environment of vigorous demand would likely result in strong inflationary pressures; or they could restrict credit expansion to try to prevent further inflation, with the result that rising interest rates would make Treasury financing more difficult and would inflict losses on holders of Government securities who had been urged to buy Treasury obligations in order to help finance the war.

System officials recognized that choosing either horn of the dilemma would result in undesirable consequences. Maintaining basically the existing rate pattern would seriously impair ability to regulate reserves and credit with existing powers. It would encourage monetization of the debt by enabling lenders to sell low-yield Government securities at supported prices and put the proceeds in higher-yielding loans and investments. The wide spread between short- and long-term rates encouraged holders of Governments to sell short-term securities and invest in longer-term Treasury issues, which afforded a higher yield and which were almost equally liquid under the policy of maintaining the pattern of rates. System creation of reserves would be largely at the initiative of holders of Government securities.

But abandoning the support policy in order that restraint could be applied more effectively would also have adverse effects. Effective restraint by traditional methods would probably result in a substantial rise in interest rates and a sharp decline in prices of Government securities. Wide fluctuations in interest rates were considered inappropriate in the postwar environment of a vast Government debt widely distributed among institutions and individuals, and large Treasury refunding operations. This view was well summarized in the Annual Report of the Board of Governors for 1945:

A major consequence in attempting to deal with the problem of debt monetization by increasing the general level of interest rates would be a fall in the market values of outstanding Government securities. These price declines would create difficult market problems for the Treasury in refunding its maturing and called securities. If the price declines were sharp they could have highly unfavorable repercussions on the functioning of financial institutions and if carried far enough might even weaken public confidence in such institutions.

The Board, therefore, does not believe that the problem . . . could be dealt with effectively by increased interest rates unless they were so high as to be a deterrent to necessary production, apart from the serious consequences to the Government security market.[1]

Possible repercussions were such as to preclude sharply rising interest rates, according to a member of the Board:

. . . the System had ample authority to deal with the existing situation by actions which would increase rates, but that in view of the vastly different conditions existing at the present time which were not contemplated when the authority was given, action by the System to increase rates would be entirely unjustified.[2]

There was general agreement that the System should maintain the pattern of rates and try to deal with the postwar situation within that framework. Several methods of providing more effective control over bank reserves and credit without abandoning the support policy were explored.

One method frequently advocated by some was more flexibility in the rate structure at the short end. With large holdings of Government securities and a broad securities market, lenders would be sensitive to small changes in interest rates. And more flexibility in short-term rates would enable the System to exercise more control over bank reserves.

A second possibility was to ask Congress for additional powers which would be appropriate in the new environment. One proposal reiterated during the next few years was authority to impose

[1] Page 7.
[2] Minutes, Federal Open Market Committee, February 28, 1946.

a special Government securities reserve on commercial banks in order to reduce bank sales of Governments. Two types of special reserve requirements were discussed: a ceiling on commercial bank holdings of long-term marketable Government securities which would enable the System to reduce or even check banks shifting out of short-term into higher-yield, longer-term issues; a special reserve of Treasury bills and certificates equivalent to a specified percentage of net demand deposits to immobilize short-term Governments and thereby reduce the need for support purchases by the Federal Reserve.

A third suggestion was that the Board might be given additional power to raise reserve requirements, the higher requirements to be applicable to all commercial banks. A major shortcoming of this proposal, however, was that under a policy of maintaining a pattern of rates, the major effect of an increase in reserve requirements would be to shift Government securities from commercial banks to the Federal Reserve Banks. Inasmuch as the System would be supplying sufficient reserves at low rates to meet the new requirement, the increase would have little restrictive effect on member banks.

A fourth possibility was a voluntary agreement with commercial banks to check further monetization of the debt. This type of agreement had proved effective at times in other countries but was not considered feasible here because of the large number of commercial banks.

TWO BASIC APPROACHES EMERGE

Studies and discussion of the implications of the postwar environment for monetary policy soon resulted in two basic approaches. There was no disagreement that it was the responsibility of the Federal Reserve to prevent excessive bank credit expansion, but there were basic differences as to how this goal might best be achieved. One view was that existing tools were not appropriate in the new environment; consequently, the Board should ask Congress for new and more suitable powers. Others, however, thought existing powers could be used effectively.

Need for new powers

Some policymakers thought existing powers were not adequate for an effective monetary policy in the new environment. In the first place, the two principal sources of inflationary pressure were a high level of income together with a large volume of liquid assets built up during the war, and a shortage of goods to meet the huge demand generated by this large volume of purchasing power. Consequently, restricting credit expansion and the creation of new money, although essential, was a relatively unimportant part of an effective over-all program to combat this type of inflation.

Second, a flexible interest-rate structure was not considered a suitable method of trying to curb private credit expansion. A moderate rise in rates would have little effect in curbing private demand for credit, and a sufficient increase to be effective would have a serious impact on the Government securities market. Moreover, trying to deal with the problem by rate action would overemphasize the role of credit policy in relation to other policies needed to combat the inflationary situation.

Thus the Board of Governors should make a special report to Congress, explain the changes that had rendered existing powers inappropriate, and request new powers that would be suitable in the new environment. The new power believed to be appropriate and effective was to require commercial banks to hold a special reserve of Government securities against net demand deposits. The expectation was that this special reserve would enable the System to maintain a pattern of rates and at the same time exercise some control over reserves.

There was some discussion of whether the System should have permanent authority to regulate consumer credit. Desirability of this authority depended in part on other methods of control available to the System and in part on the nature of the over-all program adopted to combat inflation. Policy discussions indicated System officials were about evenly divided as to whether permanent authority to regulate consumer credit should be sought.

Use of existing powers

Others were skeptical of the need for new powers; they believed existing tools could be used effectively. The large Federal debt outstanding was widely held, and the market for Government securities was broader and more sensitive than before the war. Therefore, "if some minor flexibility were introduced in the rate structure . . . it would have a greater retarding effect than in the past." Restoring flexibility in short-term rates would enable the System to sell short-term issues to absorb reserves created by support purchases of longer maturities. Thus some control over reserve creation could be restored while maintaining the pattern of intermediate- and longer-term rates.

Confidence that introducing flexibility into the short end of the rate structure would be effective was the principal argument for relying on existing powers, but there were other reasons. One was skepticism as to whether the proposed new powers would be effective under a policy of maintaining a rigid pattern of rates. Monetary restraint, to be effective, must make credit less readily available and hence more costly. The leading spokesman for using existing powers stated that for a policy to have any right to be called monetary policy or monetary control:

> . . . it must aim toward making credit less easily available and therefore more costly, and that this could not be done with a frozen pattern of rates. . . . an increase in the rate on certificates from ⅞ to 1 per cent or 1⅛ per cent would not be a large increase nor a large price to pay if it would help combat inflation, and . . . it would restore flexibility in the rate structure and get away from a frozen pattern of rates.[3]

Another drawback to relying on new powers was that getting the required legislation through Congress would likely take considerable time.

ATTEMPTS TO REGAIN CONTROL

Policy discussions from the end of the war until the accord in 1951 dealt mainly with how existing powers might be used more effectively within the limitations imposed by the support policy.

---

[3] Minutes, Federal Open Market Committee, June 10, 1946.

Those believing new powers were essential were willing to go along with using existing powers because, if proved inadequate as they believed, Congress would be more likely to grant a request for new powers. It was a period of squirming in a straitjacket—of searching for some way to reduce the amount of reserves created by purchases of Government securities required in maintaining the pattern of rates.

Modification of rate pattern

An increase in short-term rates, while maintaining the pattern on intermediate- and long-term rates, was the focus of policy discussions for most of the period until early 1951. The primary purpose was to restore more effective control over creation of reserves, and thereby over the *supply* and *availability* of credit.

Some officials believed that higher rates would make short-term issues more attractive and that investors would be more willing to hold them. The spread between short- and long-term rates would be narrowed, thus making it less profitable to play the pattern of rates. As a result, System purchases required to support short-term rates would be reduced. In addition, the System could sell short-term issues to offset reserves created by support purchases of longer maturities.

An increase in short-term rates would also tend to diminish willingness to lend. A narrower spread between short- and long-term rates would provide less inducement to shift into higher-yielding loans and investments. Also, banks and other financial institutions would be more reluctant lenders if, to obtain the funds, they had to sell short-term securities at a lower price.

Treasury officials were strongly opposed to even modest increases in interest rates (as explained in more detail in Chapter 11). They contended that fractional increases in rates would disturb the Government securities market and complicate their financing problems without having any significant influence on the demand for credit. The small restrictive effects that might be achieved did not warrant the risks involved for the Treasury.

These divergent views of Federal Reserve and Treasury officials led to a prolonged controversy over more flexibility in short-term rates. System officials persisted in their efforts to get

Treasury agreement to moderate increases. Treasury officials wanted to maintain the *status quo*. Modification of the rate pattern thus proved to be a slow and halting process.[4]

Restructuring the debt

A second approach to reducing reserve creation while supporting Government securities prices was debt management policies that would allow more freedom for Federal Reserve action. System officials in their discussions with the Treasury had long emphasized the importance of tailoring Treasury issues to attract nonbank buyers. The aim was to decrease monetization of the debt, both by increasing the proportion of new issues placed with nonbank investors and by diminishing the incentive for existing holders to shift into other investments.

The principal proposal was greater use of nonmarketable securities which it was believed would not require support. Suggestions were made to the Treasury from time to time that it would be desirable to give holders of long-term restricted bonds an opportunity to convert into an attractive nonmarketable bond. A long-term nonmarketable bond might also be issued at times to attract savings.

System officials differed somewhat as to the advantages that would be derived from nonmarketable securities. Some thought a long-term restricted marketable bond would pull in more non-bank funds than a nonmarketable bond; however, until the support policy could be modified or terminated, the possibility that

---

[4] One result of the controversy over short-term rates was the self-imposed tax on the portion of outstanding Federal Reserve notes not covered by gold. Treasury officials thought removal of the ⅜ per cent posted buying rate on Treasury bills should not be considered unless some method could be worked out for the Treasury to recapture the additional earnings that would accrue to the Reserve Banks as a result of the higher rate on short-term Treasury securities and increased cost of carrying the Government debt. Federal Reserve officials discussed three possibilities: imposing an interest charge on Federal Reserve notes not covered by gold; restoration of the franchise tax; and absorption by the Reserve Banks of fiscal agency expenses of the Treasury. Some Federal Reserve officials had a strong preference for reimposition of the franchise tax, but this would require legislation—and how soon Congress could be expected to act, if at all, was uncertain. It was finally agreed, after discussions with not only Treasury officials but certain members of Congress as well, that the Board of Governors would use its authority to levy an interest charge on Federal Reserve notes not covered by gold as collateral. The interest charge was levied early in 1947, so as to take approximately the same amount as the former franchise tax—90 per cent of the net earnings of the Reserve Banks after payment of dividends.

substantial System purchases might be required to maintain the long-term rate was a serious disadvantage.

A second objective in the System's proposals was to diminish interference of debt management operations with the timing of Federal Reserve actions. The Federal Reserve had long followed the policy of an even keel, unless the need was urgent, at the time of a Treasury financing operation. The frequency of refunding operations required in managing the huge postwar debt left relatively little time for System actions if the policy of no change during a Treasury financing were adhered to. To give more flexibility in timing its actions, System officials recommended that maturities of Treasury certificates be concentrated on four dates during the year.

EVENTS LEADING TO THE "ACCORD"

Until 1949, the System had confronted the problem of trying to find ways to restrict inflationary pressures within the limits of maintaining a pattern of rates. In recession, the problem was to increase reserves and encourage credit expansion to promote recovery.

Hobbled in recession, too

The support policy proved to be a handicap in dealing with recession also. Declining business activity and a growing margin of unused resources called for an easy money policy to encourage credit expansion and bolster total demand. With the demand for bank credit weak, banks tended to invest some of the reserves made available in Government securities. Government securities prices rose and yields fell. Under these circumstances, maintaining the pattern of rates compelled the Federal Reserve to sell Governments to check declining rates.

But selling Government securities absorbed reserves; hence the vicious circle. System purchases to supply reserves and stimulate recovery put downward pressure on market rates; System sales of securities to check declining rates absorbed reserves. The support policy proved to be a "millstone around the Federal Reserve neck" in dealing effectively with recession as well as with a boom.

The serious difficulty encountered in dealing with the 1948–1949 recession stimulated discussion as to the advisability of substantial modification of or even discontinuance of the support policy. A period when Government securities prices were rising instead of falling would be a propitious time, if a change were to be made.

There was general agreement among Federal Reserve authorities that modification of the policy of maintaining a rigid rate structure to permit more flexible monetary policy was essential. There was disagreement, however, as to how far they should go. Some wanted to get away from the support policy entirely, including the long-term rate, as soon as possible. Others were opposed to abandoning support of the long-term rate. The decision of the Open Market Committee, reflected in the following press statement released June 28, 1949, did not mean the support policy was to be abandoned; it meant only that under existing circumstances open market operations were to be directed toward maintaining an appropriate supply of reserves instead of maintaining a rigid level of intermediate- and long-term rates.

> *The Federal Open Market Committee, after consultation with the Treasury, announced today that with a view to increasing the supply of funds available in the market to meet the needs of commerce, business, and agriculture it will be the policy of the Committee to direct purchases, sales, and exchanges of Government securities by the Federal Reserve Banks with primary regard to the general business and credit situation. The policy of maintaining orderly conditions in the Government security market and the confidence of investors in Government bonds will be continued. Under present conditions the maintenance of a relatively fixed pattern of rates has the undesirable effect of absorbing reserves from the market at a time when the availability of credit should be increased.*[5]

Growing inflationary pressures

The outbreak of hostilities in Korea in mid-1950 and soaring defense expenditures increased inflationary pressures. Both a Government deficit and strong private demand were giving a thrust to credit expansion. System officials manifested increasing anxiety over their responsibility to prevent credit expansion which was feeding inflation. Treasury officials, on the other hand,

---

[5] Minutes, Federal Open Market Committee, June 28, 1949.

became more concerned about any steps that might upset the Government securities market and make more difficult Treasury financing of mounting Government expenditures.

The effect of the Korean situation and its implications were to harden Federal Reserve and Treasury officials in their respective positions. The Federal Reserve wanted the Treasury to tailor its financing program to tap as much nonbank funds as possible, and to agree to a rise in short-term rates. Treasury officials were vigorously opposed to both. According to their studies, nonbank funds would not be available and hence they were unwilling to offer securities designed to attract such funds. Neither would they agree to a rise in short-term rates because "this was no time" to upset the Government securities market.

Convinced that Treasury officials would not agree to an increase in short-term rates or to the issue of a long-term bond to attract nonbank funds, the System decided it should take immediate action to restrict credit expansion. It was also agreed that the Secretary of the Treasury should be informed of the decision and that a statement should be released to the press. Accordingly, the following statement, issued jointly by the Board of Governors and the Federal Open Market Committee, was released August 18, 1950:

> *The Board of Governors of the Federal Reserve System today approved an increase in the discount rate of the Federal Reserve Bank of New York from 1½ per cent to 1¾ per cent effective at the opening of business Monday, August 21.*
>
> *Within the past six weeks loans and holdings of corporate and municipal securities have expanded by 1.5 billion dollars at banks in leading cities alone. Such an expansion under present conditions is clearly excessive. In view of this development and to support the Government's decision to rely in major degree for the immediate future upon fiscal and credit measures to curb inflation, the Board of Governors of the Federal Reserve System and the Federal Open Market Committee are prepared to use all the means at their command to restrain further expansion of bank credit consistent with the policy of maintaining orderly conditions in the Government securities market.*
>
> *The Board is also prepared to request the Congress for additional authority should that prove necessary.*
>
> *Effective restraint of inflation must depend ultimately on the willingness of the American people to tax themselves adequately to meet the Government's needs on a pay-as-you-go basis. Taxation alone, however, will not do the job.*

Parallel and prompt restraint in the area of monetary and credit policy is essential.[6]

Even though there was general agreement within the System that more effective steps should be taken to restrict private credit expansion, there was still disagreement as to whether the long-term 2½ per cent rate should be maintained. One view was that effective restraint could not be restored without flexibility over the entire rate structure. Others believed it was essential that the System maintain the 2½ per cent rate during the emergency.[7]

What the Federal Reserve should do, in view of its primary responsibility of regulating private credit expansion and its desire to cooperate with the Treasury in so far as possible in meeting the Government's financing requirements, continued to be the major topic of discussion during the remainder of 1950 and in early 1951. The burden involved in the decision was increased by the fact that other Government officials became involved in the controversy.

The report of the Subcommittee on Monetary, Credit, and Fiscal Policies of the Joint Committee on the Economic Report issued in January, 1950, contributed to a better understanding of the problems involved. The report also recommended that a flexible monetary policy should be restored. Late in 1950, the President of the United States was disturbed by an article in a New York metropolitan paper to the effect that there was speculation as to whether the Federal Reserve was undercutting Treasury financing. He wrote the Chairman of the Federal Open Market Committee that the situation referred to was a dangerous

---

[6] Annual Report of the Board of Governors, 1950, p. 88.

[7] The basic difference of opinion as to the effectiveness of greater flexibility in short-term rates which emerged early in the postwar period still prevailed. For example, the President of the Federal Reserve Bank of New York thought that greater flexibility in short-term rates would provide considerably more control over reserve creation and hence credit expansion. Others, notably the former Chairman of the Board of Governors, favored higher short-term rates but did not think they would have much effect in curbing credit expansion. Supporting the prices of long-term bonds during a period of expansion would make reserves readily available. As previously, the former Chairman favored using existing powers available to the System other than abandoning support of the long-term rate. If existing powers proved inadequate, as he believed they would, the System should then present the situation to Congress with a clear explanation of the problems and alternatives—terminating support of Government securities or obtaining additional powers such as the special reserve plan.

one and urged that the policy of maintaining prices of Government securities be continued. He thought that with the tense international situation and mounting defense expenditures, maintaining stability in the Government securities market and confidence in the Government's credit should have top priority. Federal Reserve officials agreed with these general objectives; the only disagreement was as to the best methods of achieving them.

Early in February, 1951, there was a three-day meeting of the Open Market Committee devoted almost exclusively to what the Federal Reserve should do with increasing inflationary pressures and strong opposition to any modification of the support policy. The Committee approved a letter to the President explaining its position. The letter made four main points.

First, the System should do all in its power to preserve the purchasing power of the dollar because any policy which eats away the dollar's purchasing power would undermine confidence in the credit of the United States and the public's willingness to buy and hold Government securities. Second, the basic problem confronting the System was more effective control of bank reserves. Reserve creation had been generating a rising tide of money and there was no effective way of stemming this tide that would not reflect itself in interest rates. Third, the charge that the Committee favored high interest rates *per se* confused the issue; the objective was more effective regulation of the creation of money, which of course would be reflected in interest rates. Fourth, the System should try to work out with the Secretary of the Treasury as promptly as possible a program which would safeguard and maintain public confidence in the values of outstanding Government bonds, and at the same time protect the purchasing power of the dollar.

The Committee also approved a letter to the Secretary of the Treasury suggesting a program for discussion. The basic premise was that only by restricting credit expansion could erosion of the value of the dollar be avoided and strength of the economy maintained in the critical period confronting them. As to the specific program, the Federal Reserve would buy the longest-term, restricted bonds in such amounts as necessary to prevent them from falling below par.[8] If substantial support were required, the Treasury should offer at an appropriate time a long-term bond with a coupon sufficiently attractive so that investors would hold it, and outstanding long-term restricted bonds would be exchangeable for the new bond. The System would purchase short-term securities only to the extent needed to maintain an orderly market, and banks would be expected to obtain reserves primarily by borrowing from the Reserve Banks. This proposed program had the unanimous approval of the Open Market Committee.

There were frequent discussions, both at the staff and official levels, between the Federal Reserve and the Treasury in the latter part of February, 1951, in an effort to reach some agreement on future policies. In the absence of the Secretary because of illness, the Assistant Secretary of the Treasury was designated to represent him in discussions with Federal Reserve authorities.

THE ACCORD

An agreement on future policies was reached and the following joint statement was released to the press March 4, 1951:

> *The Treasury and the Federal Reserve System have reached full accord with respect to debt management and monetary policies to be pursued in furthering their common purpose to assure the successful financing of the Government's requirements and, at the same time, to minimize monetization of the public debt.*[9]

The agreement, popularly referred to as the accord, was designed to achieve a twofold objective: to reduce to a minimum creation of bank reserves through monetization of the public debt, and to assure financing the Government's needs.

There were four main provisions designed to achieve these objectives. First, the Treasury agreed to offer holders of outstanding long-term, restricted 2½ per cent bonds an opportunity to exchange them for a long-term nonmarketable 2¾ per cent bond. The purpose was to remove long-term restricted issues from the market and reduce the need for interim support. The System in turn agreed to support outstanding 2½'s until April 15, 1951, up to total purchases of $200 million. Second, the Federal Reserve

---

[8] Restricted as to bank ownership.

[9] Annual Report of the Board of Governors, 1951, p. 98.

agreed to maintain an orderly market in Government securities but this did not involve a commitment with respect to par on any issue. Third, the Board of Governors would not approve any change in the discount rate for the rest of the calendar year without prior consultation with Treasury officials, unless there were impelling circumstances. Fourth, the Board of Governors requested cooperation of the Treasury in seeking early supplemental legislation to enable more effective restraint on expansion of bank credit.

On March 8, 1951, System officials, after consultation with the Treasury, decided to let the Government securities market stand on its own. The Vice Chairman of the Open Market Committee said this was the first day in more than ten years that the market had been entirely without support from System open market operations. The Executive Committee of the Open Market Committee, meeting that afternoon, included in its instructions to the Federal Reserve Bank of New York to make such purchases, sales, or exchanges of Government securities, "as may be necessary, in the light of current and prospective economic conditions and the general credit situation of the country, with a view to exercising restraint upon inflationary developments, to maintaining orderly conditions in the Government security market, to relating the supply of funds in the market to the needs of commerce and business, ..."

The accord marked a milestone in the history of Federal Reserve policy. For the first time since the mid-thirties, the System was in a position effectively to regulate reserves and the money supply. Excess reserves were so large for several years prior to World War II that open market operations were ineffective as a means of fundamentally altering reserve positions or of influencing interest rates. With the outbreak of World War II, open market operations were directed toward maintaining essentially the existing pattern of rates on Goverment securities to facilitate Treasury financing. And, as already explained, inability to obtain Treasury agreement resulted in the rate pattern being maintained with only minor flexibility in short-term rates until March, 1951. The accord thus removed the straitjacket imposed by the policy of pegged rates for nearly ten years.

9. RETURN TO FLEXIBILITY— ALMOST

Under present conditions, operations for the System account should be confined to the short end of the market (not including correction of disorderly markets).

—Federal Open Market Committee, March, 1953

The return to a flexible monetary policy in 1951 confronted Federal Reserve policymakers with a new situation. None of the members of the Board of Governors or the presidents of the Reserve Banks had served in these policymaking positions for any appreciable period when Federal Reserve policy was uninhibited by either large excess reserves or supporting a pattern of rates.[1] Moreover, restoration of flexibility coincided with a general resurgence of faith in monetary policy as an instrument of economic stabilization.

Newly acquired freedom in policy formulation together with inexperience of officials in such an environment ushered in an era of study and reappraisal. Policymakers were concerned with such problems as making the transition to an unsupported Government securities market, how monetary tools could be used most effectively in the new environment, and a re-evaluation of objectives and guides.

TRANSITION TO A FREE MARKET

System officials were anxious to effect a smooth transition to an unsupported market and to cooperate with the Treasury in carrying out the provisions of the accord. The Federal Reserve with-

---

[1] Only one had served prior to the mid-thirties, a member of the Board of Governors having served since June, 1933.

110

drew support from the Government securities market in accordance with its agreement with the Treasury. By the fall of 1951, the Open Market Committee had abandoned all minimum prices at which support would be given the long-term restricted bonds; once again the market was on its own except that open market operations would be used, if necessary, to maintain an orderly market for Government securities.

Termination of the support policy required that System officials and market participants adjust to a free market. Official discussion shifted from how effective control of reserves and credit could be regained to how it should be used. Soon after the return to flexibility a policy of "neutrality" began to emerge. The meaning and tests that might be useful in implementing it were topics of frequent discussion in 1952. The major objective of neutrality was to keep Federal Reserve intervention at a minimum, afford maximum opportunity for market forces of demand and supply to operate, and encourage revival of a free market in Government securities.

How could the policy of neutrality be implemented? What did it mean in the actual conduct of open market operations? Some officials interpreted neutrality rigidly. They thought the System should stay out of the market under ordinary conditions. But the majority of the Open Market Committee thought this interpretation was too narrow. Supplying reserves needed to support an expansion in total output or to offset gold and currency flows was consistent with a neutral policy.[2] The one test of neutrality which gradually gained acceptance was whether or not an open market purchase or sale was to supply or absorb reserves.

Probing for principles that should govern open market operations led officials to consideration of how reserves should be supplied—by open market operations or through the discount window. In the latter part of 1952, a member of the Open Market Committee suggested that it would be helpful to project reserve needs well in advance. Such projections, even though necessarily inaccurate, would provide the basis for fruitful discussion of the

---

[2] One official stated neutrality should include sales to absorb excess reserves but not the sale of bonds that had gone to a slight premium, because the latter might be misinterpreted as System intervention in the market.

extent to which reserves should be supplied by open market operations and by borrowing at the discount window.

Despite the decision to abandon a supported Government securities market, System policy with respect to Treasury financing continued to be a source of concern. Federal Reserve officials wanted to facilitate Treasury debt management operations in so far as possible without interfering with monetary objectives. After a year or more of experience with an unsupported market, however, there was still some support for Federal Reserve "conditioning" the market for Government securities. System officials were afraid that in trying to facilitate Treasury financing operations the market would assume that the Federal Reserve was reverting to its former practice of supplying banks with all the reserves needed to make Treasury financing a complete success. Some Treasury officials thought that at times the System was not giving as much support as it should.

These views intensified the desire not only to avoid policies or actions that might lead to expectations or demands for more System intervention in the market, they encouraged officials to look for ways to reduce intervention. One possibility was to encourage banks to seek additional reserves through the discount window. Another was to reappraise open market policy during periods of Treasury financing. In the fall of 1952, for example, questions were raised as to whether during a Treasury operation the System should purchase maturing issues and, if so, at what premium; whether it should purchase new securities on a when-issued basis after the subscription books close; and whether it should engage in swap transactions—the sale of other securities and purchase of maturing issues. Here was another area in which intervention might be reduced.

OPEN MARKET OPERATIONS

Centralization of authority in the Federal Open Market Committee and a growing volume of open market transactions had led to suggestions, even prior to the war, that the Committee should be better informed on operations and relations with dealers. In March, 1940, the Chairman of the Open Market Committee appointed a committee of three—two members of the Board of Governors and the President of the Federal Reserve Bank of New York—to study the whole question of responsibilities of the Open Market Committee with respect to the Government securities market, as well as its relations with dealers and the market. But because of the spread of the war in Europe it was agreed that the special committee should be discharged.

Early in 1943, another special committee was appointed to make a study of relationships with Government securities dealers and the market. The Chairman of the Open Market Committee stressed that these relations were the responsibility of the Committee and should not be left solely to the Manager of the Open Market Account. The Committee should at least formulate a general framework of principles to guide such relationships.

The Federal Reserve Bank of New York was invited to prepare a statement of existing relationships with dealers. When completed the statement was to be sent to members of the Executive Committee of the Open Market Committee, which in turn would make a report to the full Committee.

In the fall of 1943, the Executive Committee submitted its report. The report approved existing relationships between the Federal Reserve Bank of New York and the dealers, but recommended that future procedures and relationships should be governed by formal rules and regulations adopted by the full Committee.

After considerable discussion, the Open Market Committee decided in 1944 to formalize rules and regulations governing System transactions with Government securities dealers. The Manager was directed to execute transactions for System Account only with brokers and dealers in Government securities who met certain qualifications. Knowledge and experience of management, integrity and observance of high standards of honor, willingness to make a market under all ordinary conditions; and volume and scope of business, amount of capital and financial condition were among the qualifications to be considered. To qualify, dealers would also have to agree to furnish the Federal Reserve Bank of New York information such as the total amount of money borrowed, par value of all Government securities borrowed, long and short positions in Government securities, volume of transactions in Government securities, and whether acting as dealer for its own account or as a broker.

Ad hoc subcommittee

Shortly after the accord, another study of open market operations, including the whole question of qualified and unqualified dealers, was suggested. In May, 1951, the Chairman of the Open Market Committee requested and was given authority to appoint a special committee to make a study of the scope and adequacy of the Government securities market and the System's relation to the market.

The study was delayed until the spring of 1952 so that it could be based on more experience with an unpegged market. The ad hoc subcommittee consisted of the Chairman of the Open Market Committee, another member of the Board of Governors, and the president of a Reserve Bank. The subcommittee employed an officer of one of the large money market banks in New York as a technical consultant.

Report of the subcommittee

The report of the ad hoc subcommittee, submitted in the latter part of 1952, dealt mainly with relations with the Treasury, with Government securities dealers and the market, and operating techniques. It made two basic recommendations of major significance for monetary policy.

Of first importance for monetary policy were the proposals regarding relations with dealers and the Government securities market. The following quotation gives the subcommittee's findings and recommendations on this point:

> *The Subcommittee finds that a disconcerting degree of uncertainty exists among professional dealers and investors in Government securities with respect both to the occasions which the Federal Open Market Committee might consider appropriate for intervention and to the sector of the market in which such intervention might occur, an uncertainty that is detrimental to the development of depth, breadth, and resiliency of the market. In the judgment of the Subcommittee, this uncertainty can be eliminated by an assurance from the Federal Open Market Committee that henceforth it will intervene in the market, not to impose on the market any particular pattern of prices and yields but solely to*

effectuate the objectives of monetary and credit policy, and that it will confine such intervention to transactions in very short-term securities, preferably bills. The Subcommittee feels most strongly that it would be wise to give such an assurance.

The Subcommittee finds two outstanding commitments that may require intervention by the Federal Open Market Committee in other than the very short-term sectors of the market, and that may add to or subtract from reserve funds available to the market for purposes other than the pursuit of monetary policies directed toward financial equilibrium and economic stability. These commitments are, first, the directive to the management of the Open Market Account to 'maintain orderly conditions' in the market for U.S. Government securities, and second, those arising from the practice of purchasing rights on maturing issues during periods of Treasury financing, and also on some of these occasions of purchasing when-issued securities and outstanding securities of comparable maturity to those being offered for cash or refunding.

With respect to the first of these commitments, the Subcommittee recommends that the Federal Open Market Committee amend its present directive to the executive committee by eliminating the phrase 'to maintain orderly conditions in the Government securities market,' and by substituting therefor an authorization to intervene when necessary 'to correct a disorderly situation in the Government securities market.' . . . The Subcommittee recommends also that such intervention be initiated by the executive committee only on an affirmative vote after notification by the Manager of the Account of the existence of a situation requiring correction.

With respect to the second, the Subcommittee recommends that the Federal Open Market Committee ask the Treasury to work out new procedures for financing, and that as soon as practicable the Committee refrain, during a period of Treasury financing, from purchasing (1) any maturing issues for which an exchange is being offered, (2) when-issued securities, and (3) any outstanding issues of comparable maturity to those being offered for exchange.

The Subcommittee feels that such qualifications as are implicit in these two recommendations would not seriously impair the constructive effect of a general assurance from the Committee that its intervention henceforth will be limited to the effectuation of monetary policies and will be executed in the very short sector of the market. It recommends most strongly that such assurance be given as soon as its existing commitments have been appropriately modified.[3]

The philosophy underlying the subcommittee report is clear. System intervention in the Government securities market should be held to a minimum because uncertainty among dealers and market participants as to when and in what maturity sector the Open Market Committee may intervene is detrimental to

---

[3] Minutes, Federal Open Market Committee, March 4–5, 1953.

"development of depth, breadth, and resiliency of the market." This uncertainty could be eliminated by assurance that the Open Market Committee would not intervene to impose any particular pattern of prices and yields, but solely to effectuate the objectives of monetary and credit policies; and such intervention would be confined to transactions in very short-term securities, preferably bills. In addition, confining System transactions to very short-term issues would minimize effects on prices and yields of longer-term securities, permit the market to reflect the natural forces of demand and supply, and furnish a signal of the effectiveness of credit policy aimed primarily at the volume and availability of bank reserves. Moreover, arbitrage transactions would soon spread the effects of operations in short-term securities to other maturity sectors.

System intervention could be further reduced by using open market operations only to correct disorderly conditions instead of to maintain orderly conditions in the Government securities market. In addition, using operations to correct a disorderly situation in the market would avoid any danger of imposing any particular pattern of prices and yields on the market. System operations in the market would also be appreciably reduced by refraining during a Treasury financing from purchasing any maturing issues for which an exchange is being offered, when-issued securities, or any outstanding issues of comparable maturities to those being offered for exchange.

The subcommittee recommended that in addition to adopting these "ground rules" regarding open market operations, the Open Market Committee should so inform the market. This assurance as to System intentions would dispel some of the prevailing uncertainty and would be especially helpful when market participants are trying to adjust to an unpegged market. The depth, breadth, and resiliency of the Government securities market would be improved, with the result that open market operations would be a more effective tool of monetary policy.

The subcommittee also thought there should be a change in the Federal Open Market Committee's procedures with the Treasury. During the war and postwar periods the Committee had followed the practice of making detailed suggestions to Treasury officials regarding types and terms of securities to be offered in forthcoming Treasury financing operations. This practice was encouraged by the support policy because as underwriter the Federal Reserve had a direct interest in the terms of Treasury offerings. Unattractive terms or securities meant that the System would be compelled to buy whatever amount the market was unwilling to absorb.

Now that the support policy had been terminated, the subcommittee thought the System should no longer initiate detailed suggestions to Treasury officials on debt management operations. Debt management decisions were the responsibility of the Treasury. Hence, System officials should provide information on current monetary policies and when solicited by Treasury officials, discuss the credit and monetary implications of the Treasury's debt management proposals.

Bills usually

The Federal Open Market Committee adopted the basic principles of the ad hoc subcommittee report. The Committee agreed that the System should no longer take the initiative in making detailed recommendations to the Secretary of the Treasury regarding specific Treasury offerings. A new approach was deemed appropriate now that the System no longer had the responsibility of supporting pegged prices for Government securities. The Secretary of the Treasury should be kept informed of the credit policies of the System and assured of the willingness of the Open Market Committee to have its representatives consult with Treasury officials when desired concerning credit policy or debt management problems.

The Open Market Committee agreed in general with the subcommittee's recommendations regarding the System's relation to the Government securities dealers and market. Using open market operations solely to effectuate the objectives of monetary and credit policy, and confining transactions to short-term securities, would minimize the impact on prices of longer-term issues and promote development of a broader, more self-reliant market in Government securities. The Committee moved promptly to put the principles of the ad hoc subcommittee report into effect by unanimously adopting the following policies governing open market operations at its March, 1953, meeting:

(1) *Under present conditions, operations for the System Account should be confined to the short end of the market (not including correction of disorderly markets);*

(2) *It is not now the policy of the Committee to support any pattern of prices and yields in the Government securities market, and intervention in the Government securities market is solely to effectuate the objectives of monetary and credit policy (including correction of disorderly markets);*

(3) *Pending further study and further action by the Committee, it should refrain during a period of Treasury financing from purchasing (1) any maturing issues for which an exchange is being offered, (2) when-issued securities, and (3) outstanding issues of comparable maturity to those being offered for exchange.*[4]

The three policies adopted in March were made, in effect, continuing operating policies in September, 1953. The Open Market Committee approved a motion that these policies be followed until superseded or modified by further action of the Committee. It adopted a fourth continuing directive in December, 1953: "Transactions for the System account in the open market shall be entered into solely for the purpose of providing or absorbing reserves (except in the correction of disorderly markets), and shall not include offsetting purchases and sales of securities for the purpose of altering the maturity pattern of the System's portfolio."[5]

Adoption of the fourth continuing policy directive did not reflect a change in the objective for which open market operations were to be used so much as an effort to prevent swap transactions. The Executive Committee at its November, 1953, meeting had authorized some swap transactions to achieve a better maturity distribution of the System's Treasury bill portfolio. Larger holdings of bills maturing early in the year would facilitate absorption of reserves created by the seasonal return flow of currency. A majority of the Open Market Committee, however, opposed swap transactions on the basis that they would create confusion and uncertainty and thereby militate against the objective of a better functioning Government securities market.

---

[4] Annual Report of the Board of Governors, 1953, p. 88; also minutes, Federal Open Market Committee, March 4–5, 1953.

[5] Minutes, Federal Open Market Committee, December 15, 1953.

By the end of 1953, the Federal Open Market Committee was firmly committed to a policy of minimum intervention in the Government securities market—a policy commonly referred to as bills only. In a period of less than three years, open market policy had shifted from one extreme to the other—from intervening as necessary to maintain a pegged market, to fostering a free market with a minimum of System intervention.

Dissenting view

The range of disagreement among Federal Reserve officials over the bills usually policy was narrower than is generally assumed. There was agreement that open market operations should normally be conducted in short-term securities which was much the broader segment of the market, and that the Treasury should do its financing at competitive rates and not rely on the Federal Reserve System for support. But there was opposition by a small minority, especially the Vice Chairman of the Open Market Committee, to certain aspects of the new policy.

In the first place, uncertainty among dealers as to the maturity sector in which the System might intervene was not considered an important reason for the alleged lack of depth, breadth, and resiliency. Instead, the uncertainty derived primarily from a flexible monetary policy and the Treasury's debt management program. Second, the effects of operating in the short-term sector do not always spread promptly to other maturity sectors; hence it may be desirable at times to conduct open market operations outside the short-term sector in order to affect directly intermediate- and longer-term rates. Third, confining open market operations *solely* to the purpose of supplying and absorbing reserves prevents use of this tool for other purposes that may be important at times in achieving monetary objectives. Fourth, adoption of the continuing operating policies, in effect, put improvement in the Government securities market ahead of the System's primary responsibility for monetary and credit policies. Finally, public commitments, such as announcement of the continuing policies, impair the Committee's flexibility to take whatever action seems most appropriate under particular circumstances. On this point, the leading dissenter expressed himself as follows:

> What I have been objecting to as a matter of principle—and still object to— is trying to write into a 'constitution' of the Open Market Committee, as one member called it, a prohibition against actions deemed undesirable by particular members of the Committee, holding particular views, at a particular time. We can't afford a freeze of ideas or practices.[6]

Supervision and techniques

The Banking Act of 1935 corrected a weakness that had previously impaired effective use of open market operations, by centralizing control in the Federal Open Market Committee. The full Committee met regularly four times a year to formulate policy and prepare a general directive to the Executive Committee of five members. The Executive Committee met more frequently and issued a directive to the Manager of the Open Market Account.

In mid-1954, another step was taken toward more effective supervision with the inauguration of a three-way telephone conversation among officials of the Board of Governors, the Federal Reserve Bank of New York, and the other Reserve Bank whose president was serving on the Executive Committee. The purpose of this telephone meeting, usually held in the morning of each business day, was to provide for a more systematic exchange of information regarding the reserve position of banks, actual and prospective market developments, and open market operations needed, if any.

In 1955, at the suggestion of the Chairman, the Open Market Committee decided to abolish the Executive Committee and hold meetings of the full Committee about every three weeks. The expressed purpose was to have a broader and more active participation in formulation of open market policy, and all Reserve Bank presidents were invited to attend the meetings. These meetings became a forum for discussion of monetary policy, not just open market policy. The change represented a significant step in policy formulation and coordination of the tools of Federal Reserve policy, even though final responsibility was still distributed among different policymaking groups.

---

[6] Minutes, Federal Open Market Committee, September 24, 1953.

The bulk of open market transactions is for the purpose of off-setting the effects of market factors such as float, Treasury operations, and currency flows. The day-to-day effect of market factors on bank reserve positions is sometimes substantial. Hence the need at times to supply or absorb reserves promptly.

In mid-1954, the question was raised as to whether it would be possible to have delivery and payment the same day the securities transaction is consummated. The regular procedure called for delivery and payment the following day. Investigation by the Manager of the Open Market Account indicated that delivery and payment the same day would be feasible, and he was given authority to engage in "cash transactions"—delivery and payment the day of the transaction. Cash transactions are especially useful when officials want to supply or absorb funds immediately.

Repurchase agreements, which had been used in the early history of the System primarily to help dealers finance their position when funds were not available at reasonable rates from other sources and to help develop and broaden the market for bankers acceptances, fell into disuse during the thirties and during World War II when the System had the 3/8 per cent posted rate on Treasury bills. Early in 1948, renewed authority was given the Manager of the Open Market Account to use repurchase agreements to supply funds to the market temporarily in periods of unusual tightness.

In recent years, repurchase agreements with nonbank dealers have been used more frequently, and the sole purpose has been to implement Federal Reserve policy. Repurchase agreements are an especially suitable tool for putting funds into the market temporarily, and when the market is unusually sensitive. They avoid whipsawing the market with outright purchases followed in a day or so by sales.

ADMINISTRATION OF THE DISCOUNT WINDOW

There was little need for member banks to borrow during the period 1934–1951, and the discount window fell into disuse. The return to a more flexible open market policy revived interest in the discount window on the part of both Federal Reserve officials and member banks. Use of the discount window came in for considerable study and reappraisal, especially in 1953 and 1954. The Board of Governors revised Regulation A, governing loans and discounts by Federal Reserve Banks, effective in February, 1955.

Review of the role of the discount window resulted mainly in clarification rather than adoption of new principles. The most significant change was a revision of the statement of general principles governing administration of the discount window. In announcing the revision of Regulation A, the Board of Governors stated that "the most important change is the revision of the foreword (General Principles) to Regulation A. The revised foreword is designed merely to restate and clarify certain guiding principles which are observed by the Federal Reserve Banks in making advances and discounts in accordance with the applicable provisions of the Federal Reserve Act and of Regulation A."

The revised statement of general principles did not make any change in uses that had long been considered appropriate. In general, these purposes were borrowing for short periods to meet reserve deficiencies, thus affording time, if necessary, to make such adjustment in assets as may be required; borrowing to meet seasonal needs that could not reasonably be anticipated; and borrowing for longer periods to meet unusual situations or emergencies. On the other hand, continuous borrowing, in effect using Reserve Bank credit to supplement the member banks' own resources; borrowing to finance speculative activities or investments; or borrowing to scalp a profit from a rate differential or to secure a tax advantage were regarded as inappropriate uses of Reserve Bank credit.

OBJECTIVES AND GUIDES

The return to flexibility after such a long lapse and in a markedly different environment led to reconsideration of objectives and guides. A spirit of reappraisal prevailed, but results consisted mainly of refinements rather than development of new objectives and guides.

Objectives

Price stability and smoothing out upward and downward swings in total business activity had long been ultimate goals or objectives of Federal Reserve policy. But severe depression and then stagnation in the thirties had demonstrated that stability in itself was not enough. Stability with a large margin of unused resources was not a satisfactory objective. Congress in the Employment Act of 1946, set up what is commonly referred to as "full employment" as a goal of economic policy.

Federal Reserve officials accepted reasonably full employment of labor and other productive resources as one of the objectives of Federal Reserve policy. In the words of one official, "the art of central banking is to approach the brink of inflation without falling in or being pushed in." He pointed out that the brink of inflation is not clearly discernible because near-capacity, full capacity, and overcapacity are indistinct. Moreover, too much money and too easy credit may lead to increases in prices instead of increases in real income even at near-capacity operations. In a practical sense, the objective was to have production and employment as close to capacity as possible without generating a significant upward movement in prices.

Neither was stability at high but stagnant levels of production and employment considered adequate. A rising level of total output is essential if the standard of living is to be maintained with a growing population. Growth as well as stability was a desirable goal.

In the fall of 1953, the Open Market Committee agreed that a policy of active ease should be continued and that "reserves would be supplied to the market to meet seasonal and growth needs, ..." Later in the year the Committee inserted into its directive to the Executive Committee that open market operations should be directed, among other things, "to promoting growth and stability in the economy by actively maintaining a condition of ease in the money market, ..." Discussion did not indicate, however, the sudden discovery of a new major objective. In projecting probable future reserve needs, allowance was made for a growth factor in the money supply, such as 3 per cent. Incorporation of growth in the directive apparently reflected only the adjustment of policy instructions to a particular phase of the cycle.

It was not long, however, until orderly or sustained growth did become an accepted and frequently discussed objective. The goal was not some specific rate of annual growth. Instead, monetary policy should be used not only to avoid booms and depressions, but also to facilitate a sustainable rate of growth in total output. It should aim at keeping total demand in balance with an expanding capacity to produce, at stable prices.

Worsening of the balance-of-payments deficit in the latter part of the fifties revived another objective that had not been a determinant of monetary policy for many years—helping defend the external value of the dollar. Thus there were four generally accepted policy objectives: price stability, maintaining reasonably full use of labor and other productive resources, sustained economic growth, and protecting the external value of the dollar.

Guides

The return to a flexible monetary policy emphasized the need for guides that would be helpful in deciding when action should be taken. Several short-term guides have been considered since the return to flexibility.

Under the policy of neutrality, a substantial part of reserve needs was met through the discount window. In fact, some officials thought all temporary and a large part of seasonal reserve needs should be met in this way. Thus the level of member-bank borrowing was watched closely in policy formulation. In the spring of 1953, for example, one of the immediate aims of policy was to keep member-bank borrowing at about $1.5 billion. This level of borrowing, it was thought, would exert about the right amount of restraint on member banks and at the same time would minimize the need for System intervention in the Government securities market. If borrowing rose above the target level, additional reserves would first be supplied by repurchase agreements; if necessary, the System would then make outright purchases of Government securities.

Using a certain level of member-bank borrowing from the Reserve Banks as an immediate guide was regarded as unsatisfactory by some officials. It was inconsistent to pursue a policy of keeping banks in debt at about a certain level, such as $1.5 billion, and then try to prohibit continuous borrowing. Moreover, administering the discount window to prevent continuous borrowing meant that maintaining a given level of borrowing over time was likely to result in increasing restraint.

Recession and a shift of policy from restraint to ease focused attention on excess reserves as well as volume of borrowing. During the recession of 1953–1954, staff members began using the term "free reserves" in statements at meetings of the Open Market Committee. Free reserves, reflecting both excess reserves and borrowing, became the principal guide used in Committee discussions in 1954.

Use of some reserve measure as a guide was the logical result of the decision in late 1953, that open market operations should be conducted solely for the purpose of supplying or absorbing reserves. Reserve measures, including free reserves, were projected several weeks into the future, and some Committee members began suggesting a certain range of free reserves as a guide for operations until the next meeting. A desire to express the Committee's directive to the Manager of the Account in more specific terms also encouraged use of some quantitative target such as net free or net borrowed reserves.

Several difficulties were soon recognized in using a free reserve target as a guide. Inability to project free reserves accurately because of wide fluctuations in such factors as float and Treasury operations made it difficult to achieve a range such as $100–150 million in daily average free or borrowed reserves, at least without conducting open market transactions that otherwise would be undesirable. The degree of ease or restraint, it was pointed out, is influenced by distribution as well as volume of free reserves. Country banks hold more excess reserves than banks in financial centers, and are likely to be less prompt in putting newly acquired reserves to work. A serious limitation of a free reserve guide is that it affords no indication of whether banks are using reserves. Use of reserves made available depends on a variety of factors influencing willingness of banks to lend and invest. Economic stagnation and fear in the thirties which led member banks to hold huge excess reserves is an extreme illustration of how environment may influence willingness of banks to use reserves made available.

There has been considerable progress since the accord in developing and refining quantitative indicators as guides. More data on bank reserve positions are available and with less time lag. Various aspects of reserve positions are considered, such as net free and net borrowed reserves, non-borrowed reserves, total reserves, and member-bank borrowing. Projections of reserve positions, and the principal factors affecting them, have been improved. Other sensitive indicators of money-market conditions, such as federal funds rate, Treasury bill rates, dealer loan rates, and dealer borrowing, are watched closely. But officials are fully aware that short-term money-market indicators, although helpful, are far from adequate. They must look beyond such immediate guides.

Reserves and other sensitive money-market indicators are only the first link in a chain of responses that may be set in motion by Federal Reserve actions. Trends as well as short-run changes are useful guides in policy formulation. A growth factor is incorporated in reserve projections to provide some indication of whether over time the actual reserve base is expanding at a reasonable rate. A change in reserve position has little effect unless it influences bank loan and investment policies. Consequently, trends in such factors as bank loans and investments, the money supply, longer-term interest rates, consumer and capital expenditures, were considered to be significant intermediate-term indicators of possible responses to actions taken and whether further action is needed.

Another type of intermediate guide which often crops up in policy discussions is unhealthy credit situations and other maladjustments. In the upward swing of the cycle, officials are alert for developments such as speculative activity in the stock market, in inventories, or in real estate. Rates of credit expansion and trends in terms in key areas, such as automobile financing, real estate, and business credit, are watched carefully. A crucial question is whether total demand is pressing against capacity to produce to such an extent that additional credit would result mainly in higher prices instead of more output.

Along with efforts to develop and refine quantitative guides were attempts to define more clearly commonly used policy terms. A good illustration of the latter was a written characterization of the terms active ease, ease, neutrality, and restraint submitted by one of the members to the Open Market Committee early in 1955.

Active ease was characterized as maintaining a volume of excess reserves large enough to assure ready availability of bank credit for all borrowing needs that meet ordinary standards of creditworthiness; the discount rate at a low level; short-term, money-market rates far enough below the discount rate so that it is cheaper to obtain reserves in the open market than at the discount window; relatively low market rates at all maturities with a tendency toward a continuing decline in rates; and with member banks borrowing from the Reserve Banks only intermittently and in small volume.

Ease is a condition in which bank reserves and bank credit are readily available to meet creditworthy demands. For the banking system as a whole, there is no need for rationing of funds among particular uses because of insufficient credit to go around, there is no pressure on banks to find uses for a continuously increasing supply of reserves. The discount rate remains at a low level; the tendency toward a decline in market rates of interest is checked; the more sensitive money-market rates, such as the federal funds rate and the Treasury bill rate, move up toward the discount rate so that at times borrowing at the discount window may be more advantageous than obtaining reserves in the open market. Individual member banks borrow with some frequency in response to expanding credit demands but a sustained and growing volume of borrowing is soon relieved by open market operations.

A policy of neutrality is one in which bank reserves are sufficient to meet creditworthy demands. Market factors are permitted to reflect themselves in reserve positions of banks which would mean in most instances no continuous cushion of excess reserves and elimination of free reserves in the aggregate. Any appreciable change in economic conditions or over-all credit demands would be reflected fairly promptly in more sensitive rates of interest, and in the event of tightening tendencies, sensitive money-market rates would be expected to move above the discount rate. Should these tightening tendencies continue, the discount rate would be moved up toward the middle of its range. There might be a moderate volume of member-bank borrowing much of the time, but continuing pressure on the banking system as a whole would be relieved sufficiently by open market operations so that a large volume of member-bank borrowing would be unnecessary.

Restraint implies an open market policy with respect to reserves that creates a general awareness that bank credit is not available in sufficient volume to meet all demands. The pressure of total demand against a restricted supply would cause interest rates to rise. The discount rate is raised to the higher levels of its range, and sensitive money market rates should be close to or above the discount rate at all times. Member-bank borrowing from the Reserve Banks would rise substantially and would be moderated by open market operations only if the apparent degree of restraint was becoming too great. Reserves continue to be available at a price. The objective is not to shut off bank credit or even bring a net reduction, but to limit growth as necessary to avoid inflationary pressures from the monetary side.

Even though earnest efforts have been made to develop short- and intermediate-term guides, policy discussions reveal clearly an awareness that wise decisionmaking is ultimately a matter of informed judgment. Knowledge of the effects of System actions is too imperfect and the environment in which the central bank operates too volatile for policy formulation by rule or formula to be effective. Informed judgment, based on quantitative indicators and all other relevant information available, is still the principal ingredient of sound policy formulation.

10. DEFENDING EXTERNAL VALUE OF THE DOLLAR

After prolonged study and discussion of the role of the dollar in the international payments system, the Federal Open Market Committee, in early 1962, decided to undertake open market transactions in foreign currencies.

—Annual Report of the Board of Governors, 1962

Defending stability of the internal value of the dollar has long been an important determinant of Federal Reserve policy. But until recently defending its external value had not been a significant influence since the early thirties.

A persistent balance-of-payments deficit since 1949 has been putting a mounting supply of dollars at the disposal of foreigners, and a return to convertibility of the major currencies in 1959 made it possible to shift funds from one international financial center to another. The continuing deficit, weakness of the dollar in foreign exchange markets, and loss of gold set the stage for the possibility that rumors or an international crisis might touch off a flight from the dollar. The Treasury began intervening in foreign exchange markets in the spring of 1961, and initiated other defenses to help maintain the external value of the dollar. Federal Reserve authorities, to help defend the dollar, terminated the bills usually policy, began operations in foreign exchange, and participated in other arrangements to help improve the international monetary system.

DILEMMA: DOMESTIC VS. EXTERNAL GOALS

The recession of 1960–1961 brought Federal Reserve officials face to face once again with the problem of monetary objectives calling for conflicting actions. Total demand, production, and employment were declining. Unemployment was rising, and the wholesale price level was stable. The objectives of reasonably full use of productive resources and sustained economic growth clearly called for an easy money policy. An ample supply of reserves was needed to encourage credit expansion, bolster total demand, help check the recession, and stimulate recovery.

But the United States was in difficulty with its international balance of payments. Productive capacity in war-torn countries had been restored with modern plant and equipment; United States producers were facing keener competition in world markets. Large military and foreign-aid expenditures abroad resulted in a substantial deficit on Government account, and there was a substantial net outflow of private long-term capital. Higher short-term interest rates in leading financial centers abroad induced an outflow of short-term funds from the United States. The deficit in the balance of payments, which averaged over $3 billion annually from 1958 to 1960, was putting a mounting supply of dollars at the disposal of foreigners. The balance-of-payments problem called for holding the price-wage line, and a tighter money policy to reduce availability of credit and raise interest rates to help check the flow of capital abroad.

Federal Reserve policymakers faced a dilemma. Should they pursue an easy money policy to check recession and stimulate recovery, or a tighter money policy to help correct the balance-of-payments deficit?

Sources of the balance-of-payments deficit provided guidelines that were helpful in arriving at a decision that would be in the public interest. The deficit did not reflect an inflated wage-price structure that prevented United States producers from competing successfully in world markets. The United States has long had a substantial surplus on goods and services; in fact there has been a surplus every year in the present century. A major part of the outflow of private long-term capital was in the form of direct investments. The large deficit on Government account, averaging around $5.6 billion annually, reflected primarily military expenditures abroad and foreign economic aid.

The deficit was not the type for which a tight money policy has long been regarded as the traditional remedy. Our substantial trade surplus was proof that United States producers were able to compete successfully in world markets. Neither were net outflows of private long-term capital and Government payments abroad the result of an easy money policy in the United States. Eliminating the deficit required a much broader program than a restrictive monetary policy. Yet monetary policy had a role to play: it was essential to prevent an increase in prices which would seriously impair our competitive position; and higher short-term rates would diminish the incentive for short-term funds—which are more sensitive to interest-rate differentials—to flow abroad.

ANOTHER RETURN TO FLEXIBILITY

In the latter part of 1960, the Federal Reserve began working toward a twofold objective: continue to supply ample reserves to foster recovery, and minimize downward pressure on short-term interest rates in order to assist in the program to reduce the balance-of-payments deficit. But supplying reserves for an easy money policy by buying Treasury bills and other short-term securities would put substantial downward pressure on short-term rates.

Departures from bills usually

In October, 1960, the Federal Open Market Committee began a series of departures which eventually ended in termination of the bills usually policy adopted in March, 1953. Seasonal needs meant that the System would have to supply a large amount of reserves to maintain the desired degree of ease; however, short-term rates were considerably lower than abroad. This combination of circumstances led the System to purchase short-term Government securities other than Treasury bills for the first time since 1958, in order to avoid putting direct downward pressure on the bill rate.

The Open Market Committee took another step away from bills usually in February, 1961. It gave the Manager of the Open Market Account authority to buy up to $500 million of Government securities with maturities up to 10 years and to alter the maturity composition of the System's portfolio by selling short-term and buying longer-term maturities. Swap transactions might be desirable should sales of short-term securities be needed to affect short-term rates at a time when the System did not want to absorb reserves.

The plan was to make moderate purchases in the 1- to 5½-year maturity sector first and later in 5½- to 10-year maturities. Federal Reserve officials stressed that the purpose of conducting operations in intermediate and longer maturities was not to set any particular level of short- or longer-term rates. Supplying reserves by purchases outside the short-term area would relieve the direct downward pressure on short-term rates and thus help stem the outflow of short-term funds. To the extent that purchases outside the short-term sector softened intermediate- and long-term rates or prevented them from rising as much as otherwise, the flow of funds into the capital and mortgage markets would be encouraged. The objective of open market purchases outside the short-term sector was summarized in the Board of Governors' Annual Report for 1961, as follows:

"... *purchasing of securities in the intermediate- and longer-term areas, as contrasted with the short-term area, offered the possibility of supplying reserves without creating direct pressure on short-term rates. Also, such purchases, by having a moderating influence on long-term interest rates relative to short-term rates, might have the effect of facilitating the flow of funds through the capital and mortgage markets, thereby encouraging the progress of recovery. Accordingly, the combination of domestic and international circumstances confronting the Committee seemed to call for a high degree of flexibility in open market operations.*[1]

The Committee agreed that its decision to depart, at least temporarily, from the longstanding policy of confining operations to short-term securities preferably bills, and not to engage in swap transactions, should be made public. On February 20, 1961, the date of initial operations in longer maturities, the Chairman of the Committee authorized the Manager of the Open Market Account to issue the following press statement:

The System Open Market Account is purchasing in the open market U.S. Government notes and bonds of varying maturities, some of which will exceed 5 years.

---

[1] Annual Report of the Board of Governors, 1961, p. 40.

Price quotations and offerings are being requested of all primary dealers in U.S. Government securities. Determination as to which offerings to purchase is being governed by the prices that appear most advantageous, i.e., the lowest prices. Net amounts of all transactions for System Account will be shown as usual in the condition statements issued every Thursday.

During recent years transactions for the System Account, except in correction of disorderly markets, have been made in short-term U.S. Government securities. Authority for transactions in securities of longer maturity has been granted by the Open Market Committee of the Federal Reserve System in the light of conditions that have developed in the domestic economy and in the U.S. balance of payments with other countries.[2]

In March, 1961, the Open Market Committee removed the restriction that limited purchases to maturities of up to 10 years, one reason being that more flexibility in open market operations would afford a better opportunity to evaluate effects of operations outside the short-term sector. The special authorization to operate in longer-term securities was renewed at each meeting of the Committee until December.

Termination of bills usually

In December, 1961, the Federal Open Market Committee voted to discontinue the three continuing policy directives adopted in March, 1953. There were several reasons for taking this step, according to official records.

In view of the United States balance-of-payments position, greater flexibility might be needed in the future in adapting System operating techniques to changing circumstances. This was perhaps the dominant reason. A second reason was that the directives which were designed to clarify the role of open market operations and thereby assist in making the transition from a pegged to an unsupported Government securities market had served their purpose. The transition had been successfully made for some time. Third, when the three continuing directives were adopted, the full Committee met regularly only four times a year. The Executive Committee was abolished in mid-1955, and the continuing directives were no longer needed as guidelines for the Executive Committee.

---

[2] *Ibid.*, p. 43.

Some members of the Committee were opposed to discontinuing the operating directives. Formalized guidelines were considered desirable even though modifications might be needed occasionally to meet certain situations. Dropping the directives might have adverse effects on the Government securities market. In any event, operations in all maturities would impair the usefulness of the market as a signal of changes in natural supply-demand conditions. Some of the opposition to discontinuance reflected a belief that the experiment with operations outside the short-term sector had not been successful. Reference was also made to one of the "classical canons of central banking," namely, that a central bank should operate only in high-quality, short-term paper.

FOREIGN EXCHANGE OPERATIONS

Early in 1962, the Federal Open Market Committee decided to launch an experimental program of operations in foreign exchange to supplement Treasury operations in foreign currencies which had been under way since early 1961. Representatives of the Committee conferred with Treasury officials to develop working relations with the Treasury and to explore guidelines for conducting foreign exchange operations.

The Committee designated a senior officer of the Federal Reserve Bank of New York as Special Manager of foreign currency operations. A subcommittee, consisting of the Chairman and Vice Chairman of the Open Market Committee and Vice Chairman of the Board of Governors, was authorized to give instructions to the Special Manager for foreign currency operations within the guidelines issued by the Open Market Committee if a decision should be necessary before the entire Committee could be consulted.

There were three principal reasons for the decision to initiate foreign exchange operations. The importance of an efficient and orderly international payments system to the United States and the rest of the free world made it imperative that the central bank of the world's leading industrial and financial power take an active part in efforts to maintain and improve the system. Second, there was need to supplement the relatively small resources of the Stabilization Fund available to the Treasury for defending the dollar from speculative attack in foreign exchange markets. Third, officials believed that the world payments system called not only for multilateral cooperation through the International Monetary Fund and other international institutions, but also for bilateral cooperation among monetary authorities of the leading trading nations. Finally, helping to stabilize the dollar in foreign exchange markets was part of a central bank's responsibility for maintaining monetary stability. Such operations were regarded as a central bank function in most major countries.

The Open Market Committee emphasized that official intervention in foreign exchange could not be a substitute for fundamental action to eliminate the United States balance-of-payments deficit; however, until the deficit was eliminated it was important to minimize the danger that political and economic disturbances might generate speculative pressures and unsettle foreign exchange markets. Treasury operations in 1961 had shown that timely intervention could do much to moderate such pressures.

There was some opposition to System operations in foreign exchange. One objection was that stabilizing foreign exchange markets was more properly the responsibility of the Treasury and it would be unwise to have two agencies engaged in these operations. Another was that central bank intervention might impair private market processes and do more harm than good.

Objectives and guidelines

In February, 1962, the Open Market Committee approved general objectives and guidelines to govern transactions in foreign exchange. One of the main objectives was to help safeguard the value of the dollar in foreign exchange markets, avoid disorderly conditions in the markets, and help make the present system of international payments more efficient. This was especially important in view of the persistent balance-of-payments deficit and large foreign holdings of dollars which rendered the dollar more susceptible to possible speculative attack. A second objective was to further monetary cooperation with central banks in other countries maintaining convertible currencies, with the International Monetary Fund and with other international institutions. Third, in cooperation with these institutions, to help moderate temporary imbalances in international payments that may adversely affect monetary reserve positions. Finally, contemplated foreign exchange operations might make possible, in the long run, growth in liquid assets available in international money markets to help meet the needs of an expanding world economy.

System officials also had more specific aims in engaging in foreign exchange operations. One was to offset the effects of temporary disturbing forces on United States gold reserves and dollar liabilities. Such operations could also be used to temper and smooth out sharp changes in spot and forward exchange rates considered to be disequilibrating in their effects.

The principal guideline for transactions in spot exchange was to cushion or moderate temporary fluctuations which tend to create market anxieties, undesirable speculative activity, or excessive leads and lags in international payments. Sharp increases in international political tensions, unusually large interest-rate differentials between major markets, and market rumors that stimulate speculative transactions are among the factors that may cause instability in foreign exchange markets.

Transactions in forward exchange are likely to be desirable when forward premiums or discounts, inconsistent with interest-rate differentials, are giving rise to disequilibrating movements of short-term funds. Transactions to supplement existing market facilities in providing forward cover may be useful in encouraging retention or accumulation of foreign dollar holdings.

Another guideline was that, as a general practice, purchases and sales of foreign exchange should be at prevailing rates.

Swap agreements

Thus far, Federal Reserve operations in foreign currencies have centered around reciprocal credit agreements negotiated with foreign central banks. Each party to the agreement is protected against loss should there be devaulation or revaluation of the other's currency while the drawing is outstanding. Swap agreements are for relatively short periods, usually three to six months, although a few are for 12 months and are renewable upon mutual agreement. As of mid-April, 1965, the System has swap agreements with 11 foreign central banks and the Bank for International Settlements. These arrangements permit the System to draw up to $2.65 billion of foreign currencies.

The System thus far has used its swap facilities mainly to absorb dollars accumulated by foreign central banks in excess of the amounts they want to hold, especially if the accumulation results from temporary forces. Exchanging foreign currencies for unwanted dollars of foreign official institutions is a means of avoiding a concentration of gold losses which might disturb confidence in the dollar. Foreign currencies, available under swap agreements, have also been sold in the market to counter speculative attacks on the dollar or to cushion disturbances that threaten to become disorderly. The volume of Federal Reserve transactions in foreign exchange, both in the market and directly with foreign central banks, totaled $1.3 billion in 1964.

As the System has gained experience in foreign exchange operations the tendency has been toward extending the maturity of swap agreements. Recently, several agreements have been put on a six-month or one-year standby basis. Drawings under these agreements, however, have a maturity of three months and renewals are limited in order that every drawing will be liquidated within a year.

System officials have worked closely with Treasury officials, both in the formulation of policy and in coordination and execution of foreign currency operations. Officials of both agencies participate in a daily review and discussion of market developments and operations in foreign exchange. Coordination of System and Treasury operations is facilitated by the fact that the Federal Reserve Bank of New York acts as agent for both the System and the Treasury in executing foreign exchange transactions.

The Federal Reserve System has participated with other central banks in promptly making credit available to help defend a currency under speculative attack. In May, 1962, for example, when establishment of the par value of the Canadian dollar at $0.925 resulted in fears of further devaluation, speculative activities accelerated the drain on Canadian reserves. The Federal Reserve System, Bank of England, International Monetary Fund, and the United States Export-Import Bank promptly placed over $1 billion at the disposal of Canadian authorities to defend their currency.

Swap arrangements, central bank credit pools, and the International Monetary Fund permit mobilization of large sums to deal with disturbing short-term capital flows and speculative pressures. The assassination of President Kennedy in November, 1963, provided a notable illustration of the effectiveness of such arrangements. There was serious danger that news of the assassination and rumors which began to circulate would touch off panic-selling in financial markets. The Federal Reserve immediately placed sizable offers of the major foreign currencies in the New York market at the rates prevailing just prior to news of the tragedy. The same afternoon, arrangements were made with foreign central banks for joint intervention here and abroad to counter any speculative developments that might occur. The mere fact that large sums were available to deal with speculative attacks seemed to help restore confidence, and initial speculative pressures soon subsided. As a result, actual intervention in foreign exchange markets by the Federal Reserve and foreign central banks was on a small scale.

OTHER INTERNATIONAL ACTIVITIES

The London gold market, which reopened in 1954, is the largest free market for gold in the world. The price in the London market is usually close to the United States price of $35 an ounce because foreign central banks can buy from or sell gold to the United States at that price, plus or minus a small Treasury handling charge, for "legitimate monetary purposes." Nevertheless, sudden speculative buying or selling sometimes pushed the London price out of line with the United States price, often with disturbing effects in foreign exchange markets.

A surge of speculative buying in October, 1960, which pushed the London price to about $40 an ounce, stimulated another form of central bank cooperation. The Bank of England, with the support of the United States, began selling gold to bring the price down to a more reasonable level. Another threat in the fall of 1961 led the United States to suggest that the Federal Reserve, the Bank of England, and principal central banks of Western Europe set up an informal selling pool to distribute the burden of gold sales to stabilize the price. An informal arrangement was worked out, each central bank agreeing to supply a certain proportion of the gold required. The Bank of England acted as agent of the group in making sales in the London market.

Early in 1962, the United States proposed that the group be reactivated to coordinate purchases when needed to stabilize the price against heavy selling pressure. Under the plan adopted, the Bank of England made the purchases for all participating central banks. The gold purchased was then distributed among participants according to agreed proportions.

The "gold pool," although on an informal basis, is now prepared to operate on either the buying or selling side of the market in order to stabilize the price of gold in the London market. It marks another phase of international cooperation in trying to protect foreign exchange markets against speculation and other temporary disturbing forces.

The Federal Reserve has broadened its international activities in other ways. A Federal Reserve official attends the monthly meetings of the Bank for International Settlements. The System is represented on United States delegations to meetings of the committees and working parties of the Organization for Economic Cooperation and Development. In addition to its foreign exchange operations and participation in central bank credit and gold pools, Federal Reserve authorities cooperate closely with Treasury officials and officials of foreign and international institutions in efforts to improve the functioning of the international monetary system.

11. FEDERAL RESERVE-TREASURY CONTROVERSIES

Large and habitual borrowers are not the best administrators of the fund to be lent.

—Nicholas Biddle[1]

The proper relation between the central bank and the Government, especially the Treasury Department, has long been a subject of debate. For this reason, Federal Reserve experience with Treasury officials on questions of monetary policy during the past 50 years is of special interest. The purpose of this chapter is to explain the important differences that arose and the reasons for the divergent views.

It would be misleading should limiting the analysis to differences of opinion leave the impression that Federal Reserve-Treasury relations is one long period of controversy. Generally, there has been close cooperation to minimize disturbing effects of Treasury operations on the money market and to time Federal Reserve actions to avoid complicating the Treasury's financing problems. Since early in the history of the System, Federal Reserve and Treasury officials have worked closely together to smooth out the impact of Treasury receipts and disbursements on bank reserves and conditions in the money market. The Federal Reserve, as fiscal agent of the Treasury, has handled a growing volume of transactions involved in the issue, redemption, and exchange of U.S. Government securities. And as for monetary policy, System officials have long pursued an even keel during Treasury financing operations.

---

[1] President of the Second Bank of the United States.

FINANCING WORLD WAR I

Meeting the greatly enlarged Government expenditures incurred in the war, together with billions of dollars of credit extended to allied countries, required Treasury borrowing of unprecedented amounts. Treasury officials were concerned as to their ability to borrow such huge sums and were particularly anxious that the first few borrowing operations be an unqualified success. As explained in Chapter 1, Treasury officials decided in 1917 to issue Treasury securities at relatively low rates, and insisted that the discount rate be adjusted in harmony with these rates in order that credit would be readily available to bank and nonbank buyers of Treasury securities on reasonable terms.

Federal Reserve officials were opposed to some of the Treasury's debt management policies. The Secretary of the Treasury initially asked the Reserve Banks to buy short-term certificates at a low interest rate direct from the Treasury. The Reserve Banks did take practically all of the first $50 million issue at a 2½ per cent rate; however, System officials were strongly opposed to direct purchases from the Treasury because of the dangerous inflationary implications. They were also opposed to the Treasury's low interest-rate policy, and were especially reluctant to establish the low discount rates requested by Treasury officials. Such low rates in time of war were considered inflationary. System authorities also stressed the need for greater reliance on taxation and borrowing from nonbank sources.

Federal Reserve authorities felt compelled to direct System policies toward facilitating war financing even though they did not agree with some Treasury policies.[2] Inasmuch as war financing was the responsibility of the Treasury and the Government, they believed it was the System's duty to help carry out the policies formulated by the Treasury.

---

[2] It appears that suggestions to Treasury officials soon came to have less and less influence. Reportedly, the Secretary of the Treasury (who was then an ex officio member of the Board) rarely attended meetings of the Board of Governors; instead, he conveyed his ideas on policy through an Assistant Secretary or one of his own aides. Sometimes he would send for a Board member to come to his office in order to impress his views on the Board. See H. Parker Willis, *The Federal Reserve System,* New York, Ronald Press Company, 1923, pp. 1222–1224.

POST-WORLD WAR I

Soon after the Armistice was signed in 1918, Federal Reserve officials turned their thoughts toward problems likely to be encountered in the postwar period: readjustments accompanying reconversion from war to civilian production; the large volume of credit built up on Government securities as collateral; and the possible impact of the network of war-created foreign indebtedness and German reparation payments on international trade and finance. They thought the Federal Reserve should continue to assist the Treasury until the war-financing program was completed; however, they wanted to restore a more normal situation as soon as practicable, in which credit would be based on short-term commercial paper arising from production and distribution instead of Government securities.

Higher rates

In the spring of 1919, discussion of a higher discount rate as one means of getting Government securities and Government-secured paper out of the banking system into the hands of investors brought immediate opposition from Treasury officials confronted with an uncompleted borrowing program and management of a large federal debt. They were vigorously opposed to any increase in discount rates or to removal of the preferential rate on advances collateralled by Government securities. In their opinion, termination of war contracts would result in a decline in Government expenditures and then loans would be liquidated regardless of the discount rate. Moreover, it was unrealistic to think the Treasury could borrow the large sums required from nonbank sources by offering higher rates. The only effective method was to appeal to patriotism.

The Treasury's opposition to using the discount rate to curb inflation is summarized in the following excerpts from a letter Secretary of the Treasury Carter Glass wrote to Chairman Harding of the Board of Governors:

> *The conditions under which changes in the Reserve Banks' rates of discount would operate effectively do not exist here today. . . . [An increase] will not result in a curtailment of the importation of goods nor in increasing our exports*

materially. In the present position of the international balances and of the foreign exchange and because of gold embargoes the Federal Reserve Bank rates cannot function internationally, and will operate solely upon the domestic situation. In that condition an important further increase in Federal Reserve Bank rates might have the effect of penalizing and discouraging the borrower for commercial and industrial purposes, thus curtailing production and distribution and increasing the shortage of goods, and consequently the price of them, and thus, in turn, stimulating speculation (An increase in rates . . . falls very lightly upon the borrower for speculative purposes, who figures a very large profit on the turnover in a day, a week, a month or some other short period.) It might have also a very grave effect upon the Government's finances. . . .

Therefore, I believe it to be of prime importance that the Federal Reserve Board should insist upon and that the Governors of the banks should exercise a firm discrimination in making loans to prevent abuse of the facilities of the Federal Reserve System in support of the reckless speculation in stocks, land, cotton, clothing, foodstuffs and commodities generally.

We cannot trust to the copybook texts. Making credit more expensive will not suffice. . . . The Reserve Bank Governor must raise his mind above the language of the textbooks and face the situation which exists. He must have courage to act promptly and with confidence in his own integrity to prevent abuse of the facilities of the Federal Reserve System by the customers of the Federal Reserve Banks, however powerful or influential.

Speculation in stocks on the New York Stock Exchange is no more vicious in its effect upon the welfare of the people and upon our credit structure than speculation in cotton or in land or in commodities generally. But the New York Stock Exchange is the greatest single organized user of credit for speculative purposes.[3]

In short, Treasury opposition to any appreciable increase in the discount rate was based on the view that it would be ineffective in curbing use of credit for speculation, would have harmful effects on business, and might seriously interfere with the Treasury's financing and debt management programs. A selective approach in administering the discount window would be more effective—a view also held by some System officials, as previously explained. It was not until the early part of 1920 that Treasury officials thought their postwar debt management program had been sufficiently completed so that the discount rate no longer need be established for the purpose of facilitating Treasury financing.

---

[3] Letter dated November 5, 1919. Proceedings of a Conference of the Federal Reserve Board with the Governors of the Federal Reserve Banks, November 19–21, 1919, Vol. I, pp. 6–8.

A difference of opinion over discount rates arose in 1923. The Under Secretary of the Treasury proposed preferential discount rates on Treasury certificates and bankers acceptances—the discount rate on all other types of eligible paper, including other issues of Government securities, to be 1 per cent higher. Preferential rates would encourage development of a market for bankers acceptances which System officials had been trying to facilitate and would help broaden the market for short-term Treasury certificates which the Treasury had been trying to develop. In addition, preferential rates on these instruments would encourage banks to adjust reserve positions in the market instead of by borrowing at the Reserve Banks.

System officials were strongly opposed. One Reserve Bank president stated: "We had our lesson once and I am amazed that the proposal should be seriously advanced again." Experience demonstrated that a preferential rate merely induced member banks to use paper carrying the lowest rate; the preferential rate becomes the effective discount rate.

Open market operations

The attitude of Treasury officials toward Reserve Bank purchases of Government securities apparently was based mainly on the interests and responsibilities of the Treasury. Occasionally, Treasury officials asked some of the Reserve Banks to buy Treasury certificates, but in general were opposed to the Reserve Banks buying Government securities in the open market. As already mentioned, the Reserve Banks began buying Government securities to bolster declining earnings as their earning assets were reduced by a decline in member-bank indebtedness in the depression of 1920–1921.

Early in 1922, Treasury officials expressed concern over the growing accumulation of Government securities in the Reserve Banks. They were afraid that large purchases by the Reserve Banks at times might push up the prices of Government securities temporarily, create an artificial market situation, and thus make it more difficult for the Treasury to select suitable terms on new issues. Once Reserve Bank purchases ceased, prices might decline. Should the terms on a new Treasury offering be established during a period of buoyancy created by Reserve Bank purchases, a subsequent decline might jeopardize success of the Treasury operation. Unrestricted Reserve Bank purchases to bolster earnings might also result in inflation and adverse effects on the economy.

System officials recognized that Reserve Bank purchases of Government securities might create difficulties for the Treasury. They took prompt action to minimize such undesirable effects. An even keel policy was suggested during periods of Treasury financing and in May, 1922, the Conference of Presidents of the Reserve Banks established a committee to centralize and coordinate Reserve Bank purchases of Government securities, as explained in Chapter 4.

There was strong opposition, however, to Treasury pressure to influence open market policy. One official stated that the Federal Reserve Act put responsibility for credit control in the Federal Reserve System, not in the Treasury Department. The System should cooperate with the Treasury, but policy should not be formulated to conform to its views or interests. It should be determined on the basis of what is appropriate for the economy and the country as a whole.

FINANCING WORLD WAR II

Except for the usual differences of opinion to be expected in a free society, the next controversy between Federal Reserve and Treasury officials over monetary policy developed during and particularly following World War II. As in World War I, Federal Reserve officials were in agreement that policy should be directed primarily toward facilitating financing the war. System authorities agreed that this time it was desirable to maintain the pattern of interest rates for the duration. But there were differences over some secondary issues, such as short-term rates, types of securities, and the amount of excess reserves that should be maintained.

Short-term rates

Federal Reserve officials wanted to establish short-term rates considerably above the unusually low levels that had prevailed during much of the thirties, a period of economic stagnation and a huge volume of excess reserves. They thought a three-month Treasury bill rate of ¾ per cent or possibly higher, as compared to the existing rate of around ¼ per cent, would give a sounder rate pattern by making short-term issues more attractive investments, thereby enabling the Treasury to absorb more liquid funds of bank and nonbank investors. A narrower spread between short- and long-term rates would diminish the incentive to play the pattern of rates and would be less inflationary. They were confident that a rate pattern with the bill rate as high as ¾ or even 1 per cent could be maintained.

Treasury officials disagreed. They favored pegging the Treasury bill rate at about the prevailing level of ¼ per cent. In their opinion, maintenance of the 2½ per cent long-term rate could be assured only by keeping short-term rates at about the same level they had been when the 2½ per cent rate was established by market forces. Low short-term rates would not have any significant inflationary implications, in their opinion, because it would be necessary to rely on taxation and direct controls to combat inflation in wartime.

Even though Federal Reserve authorities felt strongly that somewhat higher short-term rates were necessary, they recognized that primary responsibility for debt management policies rested with the Secretary of the Treasury. Consequently, they agreed to accept a directive from the Secretary as to the level of short-term rates provided he would take responsibility for the decision. The Secretary accepted the responsibility and asked the Federal Reserve to maintain the existing pattern of rates, except as he agreed to its subsequent modification.[4]

Excess reserves

Closely related to the level of short-term rates was the volume of excess reserves that should be maintained. Treasury officials insisted on a large volume of excess reserves. Inasmuch as the interest-rate pattern was established when excess reserves were large, a substantial cushion of excess reserves was the only means of assuring that the pattern could be maintained. Furthermore, it was essential that reserves should be provided in anticipation

---

[4] As explained later, a rate of ⅜ per cent was agreed on for Treasury bills.

of needs. Bankers limited their subscriptions for Treasury securities to the amount of excess reserves held. Hence waiting for reserve pressures to arise in the market during a period of Treasury financing before supplying reserves might have an unfavorable effect on subscriptions to new offerings. Consequently, Treasury officials wanted the Fed to supply, prior to a Treasury offering, the estimated amount of reserves that would be needed. They contended that large excess reserves would not be inflationary under war conditions because of direct controls.

Federal Reserve officials were opposed both to maintaining a large volume of excess reserves and to supplying reserves in anticipation of needs. They pointed out that the System could either maintain a certain volume of excess reserves with rates being determined by the market, or it could maintain a certain rate structure with the market determining the amount of reserves that would have to be created to do so. A large volume of excess reserves was not necessary inasmuch as System purchases to maintain the rate pattern would automatically create the necessary amount of reserves.

Neither was it necessary or desirable to supply reserves in anticipation of needs in order to promote the sale of Treasury securities. Banks make initial payment for subscriptions to new Treasury securities by crediting the Treasury's Tax and Loan Account; the drain on reserves comes as the Treasury transfers funds to the Reserve Banks. Thus willingness to subscribe depends on ready availability of reserves, not on a large volume of excess reserves.

System officials also pointed out that maintaining a large volume of excess reserves was inconsistent with the policy of urging banks to keep fully invested. To the extent banks accepted this advice, it was impossible to keep large excess reserves outstanding. Attempting to do so resulted in a larger proportion of Government borrowing coming from commercial banks. Hence Federal Reserve authorities wanted to maintain a much lower level of excess reserves to help minimize bank purchases, but assure banks that adequate reserves would be readily available to facilitate Treasury financing.

The posted ⅜ per cent buying rate and repurchase option on Treasury bills agreed upon represented somewhat of a compromise between the Federal Reserve and Treasury positions on short-term rates. The posted rate also shifted some of the initiative over excess reserves to the Treasury. With banks and other investors less and less willing to hold low-yielding Treasury bills, an increase in the quantity of Treasury bills issued tended to result in Federal Reserve purchases and creation of reserves. As a result, Treasury officials generally favored a larger volume of bill issues than the Federal Reserve because of the resulting increase in reserve availability.

POST-WORLD WAR II

System thinking as to policy in the postwar period has already been explained in Chapter 8 and need not be repeated here. The period from the end of the war to the spring of 1951 was one of continuing controversy between the Federal Reserve and Treasury officials over modification of the rate pattern and, to a smaller extent, over issuing types of long-term Treasury securities that would require less support.

Federal Reserve authorities wanted to let short-term rates rise to gain more control over bank reserves and thus enable them to exert some restraint. But coordination of Federal Reserve policy with debt management policy was considered essential. If the Federal Reserve permitted market rates to rise without the Treasury raising the rates on its new short-term issues, System officials would be faced with either supporting the new issue and thereby creating more reserves or being held responsible for the issue's failure.

The initial move toward somewhat higher short-term rates was made in mid-1945 when Federal Reserve officials told the Secretary of the Treasury they were considering elimination of the preferential discount rate on loans collateralled by Government securities maturing or callable within one year. The preferential rate was adopted as a wartime measure and hence was no longer needed. Inasmuch as the Secretary had just tendered his resignation, he thought it more appropriate that the question be discussed with his successor. The new Secretary of the Treasury asked System officials to defer such action because of possible adverse effects on the Government securities market and because the action might be interpreted as signalling an end to the low interest-rate policy. The Federal Reserve acceded to his request and the preferential rate was not removed until the spring of 1946.

The real controversy over permitting short-term rates to rise began to develop in 1947.[5] Early in the year, System officials agreed that the ⅜ per cent posted buying rate on Treasury bills was no longer needed and should be terminated at a time when its removal would exert some restraining influence. Treasury officials were unwilling to agree to its removal unless some program could be worked out so that a large part of the increase in interest cost to the Treasury, resulting from higher rates, could be recaptured from earnings accruing to the Reserve Banks.

There was considerable sentiment within the System in favor of asking Congress to restore the former franchise tax on Federal Reserve Bank earnings. A serious drawback to this proposal, however, was uncertainty as to when or whether Congress would act on a recommendation to restore the franchise tax. The Board of Governors, after conferring with members of Congress more directly concerned with this type of legislation, decided to use its authority to levy an interest charge on Federal Reserve notes outstanding not covered by gold. The interest charge, which absorbs about 90 per cent of net earnings of the Federal Reserve Banks after dividends, is paid to the Treasury. In effect, it is the equivalent of the former franchise tax.

Treasury officials were still opposed to removal of the ⅜ per cent rate, however. They were afraid that any rise in short-term rates might cause some Treasury securities to fall below par. The ⅜ per cent rate was finally removed in July, 1947.

From the end of 1947 until early in 1951, desirability of permitting short-term rates to rise was an important topic of discus-

---

[5] In the President's January budget message to the Congress there was a passage to the effect that debt management policy is designed to hold interest rates at the present low level and to prevent undue fluctuations in the bond market. Included also was the sentence: "The Treasury and the Federal Reserve System will continue their effective control of interest rates." According to the Chairman of the Board of Governors, the Board had not been consulted about this statement on interest rates.

sion at practically every meeting of the Open Market Committee and its Executive Committee. There was general agreement that higher short-term rates were desirable as a means of regaining more control over reserve creation and the availability of credit.[6] There was also agreement that the System's views should be communicated to the Treasury, usually by letter and personal conference between Federal Reserve and Treasury officials. System officials were also in general agreement until the latter part of the period that the Federal Reserve should not act unilaterally to raise rates without approval and cooperation of the Treasury. Treasury officials usually replied that the Federal Reserve's proposals would be taken under advisement but, often without further discussion with System officials, announced terms on new short-term securities at existing rates. This was the general procedure for many of the Treasury refundings during the period. Repeated efforts brought agreement for only minor increases in short-term rates.

The recession of 1948–1949, which convinced Federal Reserve officials that the support policy was a handicap in dealing with economic slack as well as inflation, and the outbreak of hostilities in Korea in 1950 were significant events leading eventually to solution of the Federal Reserve-Treasury controversy.

The inflation threat arising from the outbreak of hostilities in Korea crystallized instead of softened policy differences between Federal Reserve and Treasury officials. The System felt a primary responsibility for curbing inflation because inflationary pressures were being fed largely by private credit expansion. This feeling of responsibility was intensified by a statement in the President's mid-year economic report in 1950 that in restraining inflation, major reliance should be placed on credit and fiscal policies. Under these circumstances, there was no real alternative to using available powers to restrict credit expansion. Federal Reserve authorities were convinced that effective restraint could not be applied while maintaining a rigid pattern of interest rates. They proposed to Treasury officials a more effective program to combat inflation, including higher short-term rates, an increase in reserve requirements, and a debt management program designed

---

[6] For the explanation of why System officials favored higher short-term rates, see Chapter 8, pp. 101–102.

to attract nonbank funds with securities that would require less support.

Treasury officials disagreed with these proposals. Their position as to the ineffectiveness of higher short-term rates had not changed. They were unwilling to bring out a long-term bond to attract nonbank funds because their studies indicated such funds would not be available to the Treasury in any significant quantity. Therefore they would have to rely mainly on the banking system for new funds. In fact, Treasury officials, facing mounting financing requirements, were strongly opposed to any action that might unsettle the Government securities market and make their problems more difficult. The Secretary of the Treasury repeatedly stressed the importance of maintaining confidence in the credit of the Government and in doing everything possible to strengthen it. This required, first of all, avoiding any action that might inspire a belief that a significant change in the pattern of rates was under consideration. Referring to the Government securities market, the Secretary said that "every appraisal of the present situation indicates that the maintenance of stability should take priority over all other market considerations."

Meetings of the Open Market Committee and the Executive Committee in the latter part of 1950 and early 1951 were devoted largely to reviews of recent discussions with Treasury officials and, in view of Treasury opposition to Committee proposals, what the Federal Reserve could do to discharge its responsibility for credit regulation. Frequent discussions with Treasury officials and earnest efforts to reach agreement on monetary and debt management policies failed. It was only after prolonged efforts had failed and System officials were convinced that the Treasury would not agree to a program of credit restraint that they decided to act without Treasury approval. Eventually, others became involved in the controversy, including the President of the United States and some members of Congress.[7] Special meetings between

---

[7] For a chronological record of documents and events leading up to the accord see: U.S. Congress, *General Credit Control, Debt Management, and Economic Mobilization,* Materials Prepared for the Joint Committee on the Economic Report by the Committee Staff, 82nd Cong., 1st Sess. (Washington: U.S. Government Printing Office, 1951), pp. 50–74; U.S. Congress, *Monetary Policy and the Management of the Public Debt,* Hearings before the Subcommittee on General Credit Control and Debt Management of the Joint Committee on the Economic Report, 82nd Cong., 2d Sess. (Washington: U.S. Government Printing Office, 1952), pp. 942–966.

representatives of the Treasury and the Federal Reserve, started in the latter part of February, led to agreement and the accord announced March 4, 1951.

CORE OF THE CONTROVERSIES

The fact that the major controversies between Federal Reserve and Treasury officials occurred in postwar periods affords a clue to the nature of the problem. During both world wars, Federal Reserve policy was directed primarily toward facilitating Treasury financing, despite the fact that System officials favored less inflationary Treasury borrowing programs. Debt management was the responsibility of the Treasury.

Financing the wars created serious postwar problems both for monetary policy and debt management. The Federal Reserve confronted a swollen money supply, vigorous private demand for credit, and strong inflationary pressures. The Treasury confronted large refunding operations to manage the vastly increased federal debt, and an environment in which investors were much less motivated by patriotism.

It was only natural that with the war over, each group of officials considered policies in terms of their own responsibilities. System officials, although cognizant of the Treasury's problems, felt an obligation to formulate policy more in terms of their responsibility for preventing inflation instead of facilitating Treasury financing. Treasury officials, even though aware of inflationary pressures, favored policies that would not interfere with debt management operations for which they were responsible.

With Federal Reserve and Treasury officials facing difficult problems in their own area of responsibility, and with monetary and debt management policies impinging on each other, it is not surprising that divergent views developed over monetary policy. The Federal Reserve's responsibility of regulating credit and the money supply to help maintain price and business stability called for a restrictive policy in both postwar periods. But effective restraint would result in a rise in interest rates from the artifically low wartime levels. As already explained, Federal Reserve authorities were persistent in their efforts following World War II to get Treasury agreement to more flexible short-term rates, the objective being to regain more control over bank reserves and the availability of credit.

Treasury officials vigorously opposed an increase in interest rates at the end of both wars, and for essentially the same reasons. Higher rates, in their opinion, would not be effective under the conditions that existed. They would not deter speculative demand believed to be widespread after World War I; "fractional increases" would have no perceptible effect on the demand for credit in the post-World War II environment. In other words, moderate increases would be ineffective in combatting inflation; increases sufficient to be effective would be too drastic in their impact on the economy. But higher interest rates would complicate debt management and increase the interest burden of the large federal debt. Treasury officials thus ruled out higher interest rates as a method of dealing with postwar inflation.

There is no simple rule or organizational structure that will prevent the type of controversy that has arisen in postwar periods. The controversy arises from the nature of the two functions—not the institution or agency performing them. With national economic goals of price stability and a reasonably full use of productive resources, the function of monetary policy in the environment prevailing after each war was to restrict credit expansion to avoid further inflation. On the other hand, managing a large war-created debt was easier and the interest cost less if interest rates remained low and the Government securities market strong. The necessity of choosing between these conflicting policies arises from the nature of the two functions; not because performance is lodged in separate institutions.

The volume of Treasury debt management operations has grown tremendously in the past half-century. The magnitude of these operations makes it essential that monetary and debt management policies be coordinated. An understanding or mandate that both are to be directed toward common national economic goals would be a step in this direction. Low rates on Treasury securities may appear warranted if the objective is a low carrying charge on the Government debt; they do not appear warranted in a period of strong inflationary pressures if the objectives are to help maintain business stability and a stable level of prices. Federal Reserve and Treasury officials with broad economic knowledge and an understanding of each other's problems and responsibilities also facilitate better coordination of policies. The period since the accord affords a demonstration that these officials cognizant of each other's responsibilities can, in a spirit of cooperation and good will, effectively coordinate their policies toward achieving common economic objectives.

12. IN RETROSPECT

After the event, even a fool is wise.

—Homer

In historical analysis there is a bias toward being critical: one is looking back on events that have unfolded with the advantage of knowing what happened instead of making the decisions looking toward an uncertain future; and what should be done always seems much clearer to the outsider than to policymakers who must take responsibility for the effects of their actions. The "Monday-morning quarterback" may be wrong, but he is never in doubt.

The value of historical analysis is not in establishing blame, and certainly not in trying to appear wise "after the event." It is to enable us to profit from the experience of others. In this spirit the author gives his opinion as to some of the highlights and principal lessons of the first fifty years.

EBB AND FLOW OF POLICY

One of the striking features of the first half-century was the broad swings in the role of the Federal Reserve and monetary policy. The first part of the twenties was a period of notable progress; from the mid-thirties to the spring of 1951, monetary policy was relatively impotent, and the period since the accord has been one of reappraisal and resurgence.

High tide

Environmental changes resulting mainly from World War I ushered in one of the brightest eras in Federal Reserve history— the first part of the decade of the twenties. The war swept away the international gold standard, and principles developed by the

155

Bank of England were not appropriate for the institutional structure in the United States. As one official remarked, the Federal Reserve was like a ship without a rudder. Being held responsible by many for the postwar boom and depression was a strong incentive to study carefully the role of the new central bank in order to develop objectives and policies appropriate in the postwar environment in the United States.

The decision that Federal Reserve policy should be directed primarily toward domestic economic conditions instead of the balance of payments and the gold reserve was a milestone in the history of central banking. Federal Reserve officials, especially the President of the Federal Reserve Bank of New York, took a leading role in working out arrangements to help foreign countries stabilize their currencies and return to the gold standard; but in policy formulation, domestic conditions were always given priority.

The primary objective of Federal Reserve policy was accommodation of commerce and business, as indicated in the Act, but accommodation in a particular sense. Credit should be used to finance production and the orderly distribution of goods from producer to consumer, but not to build up inventories in anticipation of higher prices—to hold goods off the market—or for speculative activity of any kind, whether in stocks, commodities, or real estate. Confining the use of credit in this sense, many believed, would prevent booms and depressions and result in generally stable prices. In effect, the goal was business and price stability.

The decision to direct policy primarily toward domestic economic goals meant that new guides were needed for policy formulation. The reserve ratio lost whatever significance it had in the days of the gold standard. The search for guides did not uncover one or even a few factors believed to be adequate in reaching policy decisions. Instead, formulating policy to promote general business stability required a broad range of information as to the volume and use of credit, and the state of the economy in general. To provide the information, statistical and research functions were expanded substantially.

The intellectual ferment about policy extended to use of the tools. The discount rate had been regarded as the traditional central bank tool for influencing credit. It had been so regarded by Federal Reserve officials, not only because of tradition but also because Reserve Bank credit was extended by means of discounts and advances to member banks. Changing the discount rate was thus the principal means of encouraging or discouraging the flow of Reserve Bank credit.

Two postwar developments stimulated the doctrine of direct pressure through administration of the discount window—actually a form of selective control. Excessive borrowing by many member banks led to serious consideration of how the problem might be dealt with. Progressive discount rates were given a short trial and found wanting. Surveys and studies of the effects of discount rate changes indicated the rate was not effective in regulating borrowing by a member bank. It was not practical to keep the discount rate above commercial bank loan rates. Consequently, it was necessary to rely on administration of the discount window to prevent excessive borrowing by individual member banks.

A second and important source of support for direct pressure came from advocates of the real-bills doctrine. They believed use of credit for speculation and other nonproductive activities was the major cause of the postwar boom and subsequent depression. The lesson was that use of credit for nonproductive purposes should not be permitted to generate another boom which sooner or later would be followed by depression. The discount rate was regarded as ineffective for this purpose because an increase would not curb speculation but would have harmful effects on legitimate business. Direct pressure—refusal of Reserve Bank discounts and advances to member banks making loans for speculation and nonessential purposes—would be more effective in curbing misuse of credit without restricting the flow for legitimate business.

Direct pressure, strongly opposed by some as impractical, was a prominent issue in the twenties. Support for it as a means of selective regulation later subsided, but administration of the discount window has continued to be an important means of preventing excessive borrowing by individual member banks.

A desire to bolster Reserve Bank earnings led to discovery of one of the System's major policy instruments—open market operations. Some Reserve Banks began buying Government securities in 1921 to augment earnings impaired by the depression. The monetary effects were soon recognized. Then the System had two channels through which funds could be supplied: the discount window at the initiative of member banks, and open market operations at the initiative of the System. The flow through the discount window was regulated by the discount rate and administration of discounts and advances to member banks. Regulation of the flow through open market operations was hampered by decentralized control, but a committee was soon established to centralize and coordinate transactions of the Reserve Banks. These twin instruments of Federal Reserve policy— the discount rate and open market operations—began to be coordinated so as to make each more effective.

The early twenties was a period in which developments in central banking thought, and in policy and its implementation, were at high tide. There were rapid strides toward the role of a modern central bank: focusing policy on domestic goals; broadening the scope of objectives; exploring possible guides and expanding the information needed in decisionmaking; and developing and coordinating the tools of Federal Reserve policy.

Low tide

The severe depression of the early thirties followed by persistent stagnation undermined faith in monetary policy built up during the new era philosophy in the twenties. Many economists concluded that monetary policy was a weak reed; that fiscal policy should be the principal instrument for achieving economic stability. Policy discussions do not indicate that System officials were influenced significantly by this shift in economic thought.

The mid-thirties marked the beginning of a long period in which effectiveness of Federal Reserve policy was impaired. Excess reserves built up by an easy money policy in the latter stage of the depression, and augmented by devaluation of the dollar in 1934 and by large gold imports, seriously impaired the System's ability to influence credit. The policy of maintaining a pattern of rates on Government securities during the war and in the postwar period until the spring of 1951, largely shifted control over the supply of credit to holders of Government securities.

From the mid-thirties until the early forties, member-bank excess reserves were so large that the System's tools were rendered ineffective. The System's portfolio of securities was not large enough, even if liquidated, to absorb sufficient excess reserves to exert any significant restraint. The discount rate was ineffective because banks did not need to borrow. Reserve requirements were raised to the legal maximum in 1936–1937 to try to restore the System's ability to influence credit; but the reduction in excess reserves was short-lived.[1] Huge excess reserves was a major reason for using open market operations to maintain stability in the Government securities market instead of to alter reserve positions.

Enfeeblement imposed by excess reserves was the result of forces beyond System control. Impotence from the spring of 1942 to the spring of 1951 resulted from the support policy which the System considered appropriate. The Federal Reserve and the Treasury agreed to maintain a pattern of rates on Government securities for the duration of the war in order to facilitate financing the Government's massive expenditures in World War II.

At the end of the war, for reasons already explained, Federal Reserve authorities decided to maintain the wartime pattern of rates except for more flexibility in the short-term sector. There were three principal reasons for the decision.

A large volume of refunding operations was required in managing the huge federal debt outstanding at the end of the war. Second, traditional methods of restraint accompanied by widely fluctuating interest rates were not considered appropriate in the postwar environment of large and widespread holdings of Government securities. Credit restraint accompanied by substantial increases in interest rates would not only create difficulties for Treasury financing; policymakers were fearful that a sharp decline in prices of Government securities might touch off a wave of selling and possibly undermine the strength of some financial

---

[1] Reserve requirements were reduced somewhat in the spring of 1938 as a result of the depression but the reduction was only a minor factor in the continued build-up of excess reserves.

institutions. Some believed that intermediate- and long-term rates could be maintained; that moderate flexibility in short rates would permit effective System control of reserves and bank credit. Third, Treasury officials were vigorously opposed to any significant rise in interest rates. It would complicate their problems and, in their opinion, would not be effective in combatting inflation.

The period from the mid-thirties to March, 1951, was one of relative stagnation in the evolution of Federal Reserve thought on policy. During the period of huge excess reserves, official thinking was focused mainly on the implications of this new experience and the System's impaired ability to act effectively. During the war, System officials were preoccupied with problems of war financing. In the postwar period, thoughts were directed mainly toward obtaining more flexibility in short-term rates, and to devising some technique that would restore more effective control while continuing to support the prices of Government securities. In both respects, their efforts were largely fruitless.

Resurgence and flexibility

The accord of March, 1951, removed the shackles of the support policy and marked another milestone in Federal Reserve history. System officials were confronted with the problem of how to use their restored power and freedom. There followed an era of study and reappraisal of the principal tools and their use.

Open market policy soon moved to the other extreme of minimum intervention in the Government securities market. An ad hoc subcommittee of the Open Market Committee was appointed to make a thorough study of open market operations and their implications for the Government securities market. Within two years after gaining its freedom from the support policy, the System, in effect, put itself in another straitjacket by adopting certain continuing operating policies, including the policy of bills usually.

The philosophy underlying the continuing operating policies embodied four main points: these policies act as safeguards against using open market operations to establish or support any particular rates or structure of rates on Government securities; by improving the depth, breadth, and resiliency of the Government securities market, they make open market operations a more effective instrument of monetary policy; funds withdrawn or injected into the short-term sector soon permeate the entire market; and open market operations influence the supply and availability of credit and total demand for output primarily, if not solely, through their effect on reserves.

There are good reasons for questioning the validity of these points. Public announcement of the continuing policies tended to inhibit the Committee from taking whatever action it considered most likely to be effective under the circumstances. Evidence available thus far does not support the expectation that reduced flexibility would be more than compensated for by improved functioning of the Government securities market.

The third point—that effects of transactions in short-term securities soon spread to other maturities—is inconsistent with the main contention that adoption and announcement of the ground rules would dissipate dealer uncertainty about the impact of open market transactions on prices of longer maturities and thereby lead to a broader, improved market in Government securities. If the impact spreads promptly to other maturities, dealer risk in positioning longer maturities would not be reduced. On the other hand, if the impact does not soon spread to other maturities, confining open market transactions to short securities, preferably bills, means foregoing opportunities to exercise greater influence on intermediate- and longer-term rates. Flexibility and effectiveness of open market operations as a tool of monetary policy would thus be impaired.

The fourth point that open market operations should be used solely to supply and absorb reserves reflects too narrow a concept of this instrument. Granting that the reserve effect may be the principal one, it does not follow that marginal effects should be ignored. At times, marginal effects may be of great significance in helping to achieve System objectives.

Study and reappraisal of policy in an unpegged market led to less significant changes in other areas than in open market operations. Past policies with respect to the discount rate and administration of the discount window were largely reaffirmed. Objectives were broadened somewhat and refined. Sustained economic growth became a major objective along with price stability and business stability with a full use of resources. Guides to policy formulation were further explored and refined, but reliance continued to be primarily on a variety of information needed in formulating policy to achieve broader objectives.

The pressure of events led to two significant developments in the early sixties—termination of bills usually and the other continuing directives, and a revival of System operations in foreign exchange. The bills usually policy did not impair the System's capability nearly so much as the support policy, but it did impair the flexibility needed to meet the dilemma of trying to achieve two desirable but conflicting objectives. A policy of ease was needed to stimulate recovery from the 1960–1961 recession but low interest rates, especially short-term rates, encouraged an outflow of funds and aggravated the balance-of-payments deficit. Open market operations could be used more effectively in this situation if the direct effect on rates were diverted from short to longer maturities. Purchases of longer maturities would relieve the direct downward pressure on short-term rates, and the downward impact on longer-term rates would have beneficial domestic effects by facilitating the flow of funds into investment. The Committee abandoned bills usually and the other continuing operating policies in order to achieve the flexibility needed to meet existing and prospective conditions.

The persistent balance-of-payments deficit put a substantial amount of dollars at the disposal of foreigners and rendered the dollar more susceptible to speculative operations. After careful study, it was decided early in 1962 that the System should begin operations in foreign currencies as an additional step to help safeguard the value of the dollar in foreign exchange markets.

The Federal Reserve negotiated swap arrangements—standby credit agreements—with central banks of the major industrial and commercial countries. Foreign currencies available under these arrangements have been used primarily to absorb dollars that foreign central banks accumulate and otherwise might use to purchase gold from the United States. At times, operations have been conducted in both spot and forward foreign exchange as a means of diminishing the incentive for an outflow of short-term funds. The System has also participated with other central banks in putting a pool of central bank credit at the disposal of a foreign central bank to help defend its currency, and has joined with other central banks in helping to stabilize the price of gold in the London gold market.

THE GREAT DEPRESSION

Federal Reserve policy in the severe depression of the early thirties has been criticized by many students of monetary policy. The essence of the criticism is why didn't the Federal Reserve pursue a policy of more active ease to check the depression and promote recovery?

Official records of policy discussions indicate that Federal Reserve authorities had a pretty good knowledge of unfolding business and financial developments, but for some time they did not anticipate the severity of the decline or the developing financial crisis. Consequently, the first phase of Federal Reserve policy, adopted shortly after the stock-market break in the fall of 1929, was directed toward making credit readily available at reasonable rates to help check deflation. Discount rates were reduced sharply and Government securities were purchased in moderate amounts to enable member banks to repay some of their indebtedness. In the second phase of depression policy—the spring of 1932 to the spring of 1933—the objective shifted to building up excess reserves in order to encourage banks to expand their loans and investments. Finally, following the banking holiday in March, 1933, the program of buying Government securities was resumed but as a means of cooperating with the Government's national economic recovery program instead of supplying more reserves *per se*. This program was terminated in the fall of 1933.

Now, as to why policymakers did not pursue a more aggressive policy of ease. An important reason was the theory some policymakers still held as to the nature and causes of depression. Orderly liquidation of speculative credit built up during the boom was considered a prerequisite for sound recovery. Others believed the depression was largely the result of excess capacity and overproduction. Too much ease would not be helpful; it might retard or even prevent the liquidation and readjustments required for enduring recovery.

A second reason was general agreement that recovery should be sought within the framework of the gold standard. As depression deepened, the majority favored more ease and early in 1931 a threefold program was agreed on: further reduction in discount rates, lower buying rate on acceptances, and additional purchases of Government securities. Heavy deposit withdrawals continued, and in the fall of 1931 this internal drain was aggravated by an outflow of gold. The drain on gold reserves was met in the traditional way—an increase in the discount rate. Protecting the reserve and safeguarding the gold standard was the principal reason for the temporary tightening in the fall of 1931.

A third and closely related reason was that responsibility began to weigh heavily on some officials, especially Reserve Bank presidents, as continued cash withdrawals seriously impaired the reserve position of some Reserve Banks. Some of the presidents became seriously concerned over the ability of their Reserve Banks to assist member banks facing runs and to meet other possible emergency needs. There was general agreement that the Reserve Banks should be liberal in extending credit to banks facing runs. Banking policy, as it was often referred to in those days, had become more important in the opinion of some than monetary policy. But as reserve positions became more precarious, officials faced a dilemma: should dwindling reserves be conserved in order to be able to make advances and to issue Federal Reserve notes to member banks facing runs and for other possible emergencies; or should the Reserve Banks purchase more Government securities in the hope that deflation would be arrested and conversion of deposits into cash curtailed?

Government securities purchases usually resulted in a reduction of member-bank indebtedness to the Reserve Banks and therefore less eligible commercial paper was available as collateral for Federal Reserve notes. A shortage of eligible paper meant that the Reserve Banks had to substitute gold as collateral in order to issue notes. Impaired ability to issue notes was serious at a time when member banks were facing runs. The presidents of some Reserve Banks, with little free gold left, refused to participate in purchasing additional Government securities. Legislation early in 1932 permitted Government securities as collateral behind Federal Reserve notes and relieved much of the anxiety over the diminishing supply of reserves and eligible paper. Open market purchases were stepped up, and maintaining excess reserves of $250 million to $300 million became an objective of open market policy about mid-1932.

A fourth factor that discouraged a more aggressive open market policy as the depression deepened was the tendency of banks to build up excess reserves. The build-up of excess reserves was regarded by some as evidence of the futility of buying more Government securities until banks used the reserves already supplied. Only a minority thought building up excess reserves would sooner or later put enough pressure on banks to stimulate credit expansion.

Appraising policy formulation during such a severe depression involves the problem of visualizing the situation in the perspective of the times. The discount rate of the Federal Reserve Bank of New York was reduced from 6 per cent in October, 1929, to 2½ per cent in June, 1930, and to 1½ per cent by May, 1931. Discounts and advances to member banks, which totaled around $1 billion prior to the onset of the depression, averaged a little more than $300 million in the first half of 1930, and declined to about $230 million in the second half. Prior to the early thirties the discount window was the principal source of reserves. Rates on short-term commercial paper dropped from over 6 per cent in the fall of 1929 to less than 3 per cent by the end of 1930 and to 2 per cent by mid-1931. Excess reserves averaged $62 million in the second half of 1930; $99 million in the second half of 1931; and $377 million in the second half of 1932. These amounts seem small, but in relation to required reserves were the equivalent, as of January, 1965, to excess reserves of $550 million, $975 million, and $4,300 million, respectively.

Federal Reserve authorities did pursue a policy of ease, according to the principal indicators of conditions in the money and credit markets. Whether more aggressive ease initiated earlier would have arrested the depression or substantially diminished its severity cannot be proved or disproved. There were unusually deepseated forces at work—depressed conditions in agriculture and a substantial number of bank failures in the twenties, and runs on reserves in leading financial centers abroad in 1931. From the vantage point of hindsight, it appears that more aggressive ease in the early part of the depression would have been helpful; however, it is doubtful that it would have substantially dulled the impact of an unusual conjuncture of forces tending to produce financial crisis and severe depression.

WAR FINANCING

In both world wars, Federal Reserve policy was directed primarily toward facilitating the huge volume of Treasury operations required in financing Government expenditures. There were good reasons. The spirit of the times was that all efforts, including those of the Federal Reserve, should be channeled toward winning the war. Preventing inflation in wartime, although desirable, was regarded by System officials as mainly the responsibility of Government through its fiscal and debt management policies, and direct controls over prices, wages, and materials. Federal Reserve officials conferred with Treasury officials on war financing programs, but final decision for fiscal and debt management policies rested with the Treasury.

Treasury borrowing in both wars was at unusually low rates. Although the mechanics differed, Federal Reserve policy made Reserve Bank credit readily available at the low rates. War financing resulted in the build-up of a vast amount of purchasing power which, once direct controls were removed, generated sharply rising prices and inflation.

At the end of each war, Federal Reserve officials were confronted with the same dilemma: maintain low rates to facilitate large postwar Treasury financing operations and to avoid possible serious repercussions from sharply declining prices of Government securities thus continuing to feed the inflationary boom; or apply effective restraint which by raising interest rates would complicate the Treasury's debt management problems and inflict losses on many investors who bought Government securities at low rates to help finance the war. |

There is no easy answer to this dilemma; however, three questions deserve serious study. First, is it really in the public interest to finance a war at unusually low rates of interest? Good reasons were given for low rates, a major one being to help hold down the cost of the wars. War expenditures are so huge that savings wherever possible seem important. But more attention should be given to the longer-run effects. Interest cost on the debt was only 3 per cent of total Government expenditures during the period 1942 to 1945, inclusive. Higher interest rates on Treasury securities would have made the securities more attractive and stimulated additional nonbank purchases; less promotional and sales efforts probably would have been needed to sell the securities.

| Much more important, however, is the problem created for the postwar period. Financing a war at low interest rates may give an illusion of economy but the price in other respects may be high. Maintaining in World War II an interest rate pattern established in a period of economic stagnation and large excess reserves contributed to a large increase in the money supply which was unleashed as soon as direct controls were removed. Effective monetary restraint at the end of the war on further expansion would have resulted in rising interest rates and a reduction in artificial capital values based on the low wartime rates. Maintaining the rate pattern turned the Federal Reserve into an "engine of inflation," feeding further upward turns in the wage-price spiral. Hardships imposed by choosing either horn of this dilemma were really a part of the cost of the low interest rate policy followed in financing the war. This dilemma could be avoided only by financing a war at an interest rate structure that would be appropriate in a noninflationary postwar environment of vigorous aggregate demand. |

A second question which merits serious consideration is whether it is in the public interest for the central bank to adopt wartime policies that in effect put reserve creation at the initiative of the market. In practice, maintaining any rigid pattern of rates, as in World War II, amounts to posting fixed buying rates for key maturities of Government securities. Perhaps some program of

Treasury borrowing to finance a war could be developed that would enable the Federal Reserve to facilitate the borrowing program without putting Reserve Bank credit on tap at low rates.

A third question, in the event war financing has been at low rates, is whether over-all public interest is better served by maintaining the low rates to assist the Treasury and to avoid repercussions from declining Government securities prices, or by exerting enough restraint to avoid further inflation. Looking back, it appears that in both postwar periods, Federal Reserve authorities overestimated the dangers and hardships that would be imposed by effective restraint and the resulting rise in interest rates; they underestimated the inflationary impact of maintaining the low wartime rates in the postwar environment. Experience indicates that hardships imposed by an inflationary rise in prices of goods and services are probably greater than the burden of higher interest costs and capital losses to holders of outstanding fixed-income securities. A general rise in prices of goods and services is a high price tag for maintaining stable Government securities prices and low interest rates.

ROLE OF RESEARCH

The art of central banking has been described as "reaching adequate conclusions from inadequate facts." Lack of adequate information became much more obvious when the objective of policy shifted from protecting the gold reserve to domestic economic stability.

This shift in objectives accelerated development and expansion of the research and statistics functions in order to provide the greater amount of information needed in policymaking. And as policy objectives became broader in scope, the larger the amount of information needed for sound policy decisions. One of the principal tasks of the research function has been to provide statistics and other information for policy formulation. The growing size and complexity of the economy has put increasing demands on research.

The contribution of research to wise policy decisions extends beyond information-gathering. Diagnosis of the data and implications of recent developments for Federal Reserve policy are also needed by policymakers. Keeping abreast of economic developments and analyzing their significance for policy is a major function of professional economists. Both the Board and the Reserve Banks enlarged their staffs of economists, especially in the past 25 years, to provide analytical information that would be useful in formulating monetary policy.

Theoretical analysis is one of the principal reasons policymakers, provided with the same data and other types of economic information, often come out with different diagnoses and decisions as to policy that should be pursued.

Central bankers confront somewhat the same type of problem as the practicing physician. He first gathers relevant information in order to diagnose the state of his patient's health. Then, drawing on his knowledge of medical science, he prescribes treatment. His ability to prescribe an effective remedy is limited by the state of development of medical science as well as by the amount of relevant information for diagnosis.

The real-bills doctrine provides an outstanding illustration of the role of theory in Federal Reserve policy formulation. One of the principles underlying the Federal Reserve Act was that extension of Reserve Bank credit, whether in the form of Federal Reserve notes or discounts and advances to member banks, should be by means of short-term, self-liquidating commercial paper. This type of paper, according to the doctrine, would expand and contract with the volume of legitimate business, i.e., the volume of production and orderly marketing of goods. Reserve Bank credit would thus respond to changes in the volume of business activity. Consequently, confining credit to productive uses would automatically result in the proper quantity of credit. Advocates of the real-bills doctrine thus favored direct pressure to regulate certain uses of credit instead of the discount rate which affected the total quantity of credit.

Experience gradually disproved the basic principles of the real-bills doctrine. The quality of paper discounted or put up as collateral for an advance from a Reserve Bank had no effect whatever on use of the proceeds. More important, attempts to confine credit to productive uses did not result in an appropriate total quantity of credit. Credit extended for productive use could expand beyond capacity to produce and thus help generate inflation; a shortage of eligible commercial paper in the Great Depression handicapped the Reserve Banks and contributed to deflation. Even though unsound in principle, the theory was an important influence in policy formulation in the first two decades of the Federal Reserve System.

The depressions of 1920–1921 and 1929–1933 also illustrate the influential role of theory. In the latter part of 1920, Federal Reserve authorities thought that a depression was developing. But it was generally regarded as the inevitable aftermath of the war and postwar boom. Moreover, they believed that excesses generated during the boom, such as large-scale use of credit for speculative and nonproductive purposes, top-heavy inventories, and inflated prices had to be removed in order to establish the basis for sound recovery. Hence the policy prescription of lending freely at high rates to promote orderly liquidation. Lending freely was the means of avoiding forced liquidation and its resulting losses and hardships. High rates would encourage orderly liquidation as funds became available for repayment and would discourage extending new loans for wasteful and nonproductive purposes. Granting this theory of depression, which at the time was widely held outside as well as inside the System, Federal Reserve officials prescribed the appropriate policy.

Some policymakers thought depression was caused mainly by nonmonetary factors such as excess capacity and overproduction. They vigorously opposed aggressive ease to stimulate recovery on the basis that it would not be helpful and might retard recovery by encouraging further expansion of capacity and by hampering readjustments essential for a healthy recovery.

Effectiveness of central bank policy is limited more by inadequate development of monetary theory than by lack of ability to diagnose the health of the economy. Economists disagree as to the role of money and credit in maintaining stability and sustained growth, and as to the channels through which Federal Reserve actions influence total spending and the price level. Some stress the quantity of money, some interest rates, and others regard liquidity as the "centerpiece" of monetary policy. The art of central banking might well be defined as trying to apply a confusion of theories to an ever-changing economy to achieve socially accepted objectives.

DECISIONMAKING PROCESS

The task of policy formulation has become increasingly complex as objectives have broadened and as the economy has become more and more intricate. In earlier years, policymakers searched for rules or formulas that would simplify the task. But experience indicates there is no substitute for discretion.

Rules and rigidities have never been reliable methods of reaching sound policy decisions. Under the international gold standard prior to World War I, the reserve ratio was presumed by many to provide an automatic signal for central bank action. In 1920, four Reserve Banks adopted progressive discount rates as a means of preventing excessive member-bank borrowing. Progressive rates proved unsatisfactory and were soon abandoned. Maintaining the pattern of rates for several years after World War II and continuing operating policies, including bills usually, governing open market operations were other notable illustrations of rigidities that interfered with the flexibility of Federal Reserve policy.

Rules and rigidities, whether to serve as an automatic means of implementing policy or merely to inhibit change, are inherently unsound. The implication is that policy can be better formulated for future conditions that cannot be foreseen than when policymakers confront the problem and have all available information about the specific situation. At best, rigidities become imbedded in official thinking and tend to inhibit freedom of action.

Flexibility in thought as well as action is essential for effective policy. The Federal Reserve System operates in an institutional, economic, and social environment that is constantly changing. The reason judgment is essential in policy formulation was well expressed in the following quotation given by a former System official:

We can be certain that reliance upon any simple rule or set of rules would be dangerous. Economic situations are never twice alike. They are compounded of different elements—foreign and domestic, agricultural and industrial, monetary and nonmonetary, psychological and physical—and these various elements are combined in constantly shifting proportions.[2]

Informed judgment, based on all germane information available, statistical and analytical, is an essential ingredient of policy formulation.

Policy in the Federal Reserve System is formulated by the Board of Governors and the presidents of the Reserve Banks instead of by one person or small group. To the management expert, the decisionmaking process probably appears too decentralized and unwieldy. It is somewhat cumbersome and is not so conducive to prompt, decisive action as when authority is highly centralized. Federal Reserve history reveals several instances in which strongly divergent views among officials contributed to delay and compromise actions.

But there are offsetting advantages, especially for an institution with the responsibility of formulating policy solely in the public interest. The policymaking procedure taps a broad cross section of views—public and private, producer and consumer, borrower and lender, professional economists and men actually engaged in a variety of economic activities. This blending of a wide variety of views is an appropriate procedure for the formulation of national monetary policy. It assures that practically every conceivable angle of a problem will be brought to the attention of the policymakers before a final decision is made. Moreover, the distribution of authority is a safeguard against the inherent tendency for one's viewpoint to be influenced by the prevailing attitude and environment in which he lives and works, whether the securities market, politics or government. In this connection, it is reassuring that the minutes of policy discussions show that Federal Reserve officials—whether members of the Board of Governors or a Reserve Bank president—have been motivated by the public interest, not by private or regional interests. This is as it should be.

---

[2] Allyn A. Young, Harvard University, quoted by Allan Sproul in "The Federal Reserve System—Working Partner of the National Banking System for Half a Century," in *Banking and Monetary Studies*, Deane Carson, Editor (Homewood, Illinois: Richard D. Irwin, Inc., 1963), p. 68.

The democratic process of frank and free discussion by informed and responsible men is much less likely to lead to colossal blunders than vesting authority in one man. The disadvantages of the democratic process, whether in formulating central bank policy or in running a government, are part of the price we pay for safeguards against possibly erratic and irresponsible decisions that sometimes result from highly centralized control.

RELATION TO THE GOVERNMENT

The first fifty years of Federal Reserve history reveal, paraphrasing Nicholas Biddle, that a large and habitual borrower is not a good administrator of the institution that creates the money. The major controversies between the Federal Reserve and the Treasury over monetary policy have always found the Treasury on the side of lower rates and less restraint. This is not surprising. Responsibility for borrowing and managing a large federal debt provides an inducement to support a monetary policy that facilitates the Treasury's financial operations. So it is with private control. There is an inducement to slant policy toward private instead of the national interest. Control by a large borrower, public or private, results in a conflict of interest.

The crucial question is what arrangement is most likely to result in Federal Reserve policy being formulated effectively and solely in the interest of the country as a whole. For the central bank to be most effective in contributing to the achievement of national economic goals, policy formulation should be in the hands of qualified and experienced central bankers.

To provide an environment conducive to formulating policy solely in the public interest, these central bankers should be insulated from both political and private pressures. The need for independence from political pressure was stressed by Carter Glass after he had served as Secretary of the Treasury and ex officio Chairman of the Board of Governors, and as a member of Congress:

Moreover, I commend, without qualification of any description, as worthy of emulation Mr. Wilson's wise determination to refrain from executive interference with federal reserve administration and his refusal to permit politics to become a factor in any decisions taken. Unless the example thus set by President Wilson shall be religiously adhered to, the system, which so far has proved a benediction to the nation, will be transformed into an utter curse. The political pack, regardless of party, whether barking in Congress or burrowing from high official station, should be sedulously excluded.[3]

It is equally important that System officials not be subject to undue private influence. The organizational structure of the Federal Reserve System reflects attempts of Congress to protect Federal Reserve policymakers from either undue private or political pressures.

This arrangement does not mean independence *from* Government. Congress in creating the Federal Reserve System provided a comprehensive legal framework governing its operations and amends this framework as it sees fit. Congress also requires periodic reports covering the System's policy actions and operations. But within this legal framework, Federal Reserve officials are given sufficient freedom to formulate policies that in their judgment will best contribute to achievement of national economic goals such as business and price stability, and sustained economic growth. It is logical that Federal Reserve authorities, with training and experience in central banking, are better qualified than other officials to determine Federal Reserve actions needed to achieve such economic objectives.

---

[3] H. Parker Willis, *The Federal Reserve System* (New York: The Ronald Press Co., 1923), p. ix.

EPILOGUE

The past is prologue. The future rests in our hands.

—Anonymous

Historically, central banking is young. Most of the progress made, both in terms of the number of central banks and more significantly in the scope of their policies and responsibilities, has been in the past fifty years. It was in this era that central banking began to play an influential role in helping achieve important domestic economic objectives. Developments in this period pave the way for even greater progress in the next fifty years.

But as the focus shifts from past to future, one's vision becomes blurred and confidence gives way to diffidence. It is impossible to foretell the evolution and major developments in monetary policy in the next half-century. Past experience, however, indicates policy functions and responsibilities of the Federal Reserve System will be shaped mainly by the environment in which the System operates and the quality of its leadership.

ENVIRONMENTAL FACTORS

It is certain that environment—economic, political, and social— will exercise a substantial influence on the role and effectiveness of Federal Reserve policy. It is also certain that one cannot now visualize even the more sweeping environmental changes of the future. Nevertheless, some surmises as to changes likely to impinge on the future role of monetary policy seem plausible.

Toward "One World"

The trend since World War II toward closer economic ties among countries of the free world is unlikely to be reversed, except possibly temporarily. Developed countries are taking a more active part in aiding underdeveloped countries. Modern transportation and communication have diminished drastically the barrier of

175

distance; the physical barriers to one world are shrinking at a rapid pace. Removal and liberalization of controls and convertibility of major currencies permit a freer flow of goods and capital among free-world countries.

Closer international economic relations are likely to have diverse effects on monetary policy. Currency convertibility, and a wider use of the dollar in international payments and as a reserve currency, render the dollar more susceptible to interest-rate differentials, and international tension. Some form of defensive action may be required more frequently than in the past.

Recent developments in the international field have tended to impair the effectiveness of Federal Reserve policy in defending the external value of the dollar. The deficit in the United States balance of payments arises largely from transactions unrelated or only remotely related to market forces. The large deficit on Government account—mostly military expenditures abroad and foreign aid—is determined by noneconomic objectives. A substantial part of the net outflow of private long-term capital is in the form of direct investments, and is not closely related to interest-rate differentials. A tight money policy is not so effective for this type of balance-of-payments deficit as for the traditional one arising from excess demand, rising prices, and a trade deficit.

The balance-of-payments situation, widespread use of the dollar as a reserve currency, and increasing international mobility of short-term capital may result in the Federal Reserve being handicapped more than formerly in using its tools to achieve domestic economic goals. Short-term funds have become more sensitive to international interest-rate differentials. With foreign exchange rates permitted to fluctuate only within narrow limits, the burden of adjustment to interest-rate differentials tends to fall on a flow of funds from lower to higher interest-rate financial centers. With exchange rates pegged, actions to narrow interest-rate differentials or some form of selective control are the remaining methods of dealing with a persistent and sizable outflow of short-term funds. It could be that we may be confronted with choosing between more flexibility in monetary policy or more flexibility in foreign exchange rates, such as permitting a somewhat wider range of fluctuation above and below par.

Fiscal and other Government policies

Another change that appears likely is a more effective use of fiscal and other Governmental policies to help achieve general economic objectives. Built-in stabilizers, such as a progressive income tax and unemployment insurance, are an important step in this direction. Recent tax cuts to facilitate continued economic growth, the proposal that the President be given standby authority to make limited changes in income-tax rates, and the announced guidelines for wage and price policies are indications that fiscal and other Government policies may be slanted more toward stabilization and growth objectives. To the extent this occurs, the burden on monetary policy may be reduced. Perhaps in the future there will be less discussion of whether monetary *or* fiscal policy should be the principal stabilization weapon, and more discussion of what *mix* is best suited to a particular situation.

Role of money and credit

Money and credit are the *raison d'être* of central banking. The pervasiveness of policy depends significantly on the role of money and credit in the economy. In underdeveloped countries, for example, central banks often have little influence because use of money and credit is confined to a fairly small segment of total economic activity, and the money supply is influenced more by the government's fiscal policy and the balance of payments than by expansion and contraction of bank credit.

Use of money and credit in the United States has increased substantially in the past five decades. Extension of specialization and production for the market place resulted in money being used as a medium of exchange for the bulk of total output. Use of credit, once confined largely to producers, is now widely used by consumers for purchase of durable goods and real estate.

In the future, more of the changes are likely to take the form of a more intensive use rather than use being extended to other segments of the economy. Credit terms are likely to be better tailored to borrower needs, and credit may be used for more purposes. Mechanics of effecting payment will probably change drastically. An expert in the field recently predicted that within

25 years or so "automated credit will replace checks as the prime medium of exchange." Innovations are also likely in the intermediary function of mobilizing savings and allocating them among alternative investments.

But regardless of the innovations that may come in the mechanics of effecting payment and in performing the intermediary function, so long as credit remains a device for spending tomorrow's income for today's output it will probably contribute to fluctuations in purchasing power. If so the role of monetary policy will be undiminished, but implementation may well be more complicated.

Monetary theory

History demonstrates that monetary theory has a major influence on Federal Reserve policy. But with the present status of theory, the central banker confronts two major difficulties.

The first is a confusion of theories. Some of our best known academic economists advocate a constant rate of growth in the money supply; others stress interest rates and the availability of credit. The report of the Radcliffe Committee on the British monetary system of a few years ago concluded that liquidity, not the money supply, should be the centerpiece of central bank policy.

There is also basic disagreement among economists as to whether monetary policy can be effective in stabilizing shorter-run swings in business activity. Some think it can and should be so used; others think it cannot and therefore should be used only for long-run stabilization.

Which theory or combination of theories should Federal Reserve authorities try to implement? Policy, even though adeptly implemented, will not be effective if based on an erroneous theory. Unfortunately, there is no *proof* that current theories are more accurate than those that motivated Federal Reserve policies in the twenties and the Great Depression—policies now severely criticized by many economists.

A second difficulty is that theories are formulated on the basis of certain premises and the assumption that other things remain the same. The central banker, however, is compelled to formulate and implement policy in a world in which economic conditions never remain the same. Economic theory, to be helpful in policymaking, should be applicable to the economy in which we live—not an unreal and static economy erected on assumptions.

The unsatisfactory state of development of theory is one of the more severe limitations on effectiveness of Federal Reserve policy. Despite the difficulties that abound, progress can and will be made in further development of monetary theory. Such development should be given top priority and approached from two angles: intensive study of the effects of Federal Reserve actions which may reveal certain general principles at work; and efforts to achieve further development and refinement of theory, using our growing volume of data and improved statistical techniques to test their validity. History demonstrates that basic research is one of the more fruitful avenues to economic and social progress.

FEDERAL RESERVE PERFORMANCE

The role of the Federal Reserve and the potency of its policies will also be appreciably affected by the skill with which policy is formulated and implemented.

Objectives and implementation

The future may well bring new objectives of Federal Reserve policy. In any event, shifts in the weight given current goals are likely to occur.

Policy may not be oriented so much toward smoothing out business fluctuations—the dominant goal during most of the first fifty years. Built-in stabilizers, improved inventory control, better understanding of the business cycle by businessmen, and improved use of Government policies to maintain stability may result in some diminution in the intensity of cyclical swings as well as a stabilization program that puts less responsibility on monetary policy.

As already pointed out, current trends indicate that international activities of the Federal Reserve may be more important than in the first fifty years.

In recent years, sustained economic growth has become one of the major explicit objectives but has not been a dominant influence in policy formulation. The prevailing view among policymakers has been that in trying to maintain price stability and a full use of resources the System at the same time was pursuing the policy best suited to facilitate sustained economic growth. In our present state of knowledge, this view appears plausible. But too little is known about determinants of economic growth. Additional knowledge might reveal that monetary policy could make a more positive contribution.

One of the more fruitful potentials is a more refined use of the tools of Federal Reserve policy. Except for stock-market credit and temporary authority to regulate consumer and real-estate credit, policy during the past three decades has been directed primarily toward altering the total quantity of credit and aggregate demand. The recent dilemma of business recession and a serious balance-of-payments deficit inspired attempts to achieve selective effects within the policy of general ease to promote recovery and expansion. Reserves were supplied in ways to divert the direct downward impact from short- to longer-term rates. Lifting the ceiling on rates commercial banks could pay on time deposits tended to put upward pressure on short-term rates; in addition, there may have been some stimulative effect on the flow of saving and rate of investment.

A more adept use of general quantitative tools might enable the System to achieve selective as well as aggregate effects. This is an area that needs further study and exploration. Improved knowledge of the effects of the different tools might make possible the blending of various selective impacts with general ease or restraint, a capability that would be especially helpful when objectives call for conflicting actions.

Leadership the key

Past history teaches that leadership will provide the key as to how well the Federal Reserve System functions in the coming decades. The legal framework under which most central banks operate affords a large measure of flexibility. Hence the role of a central bank is determined largely by the vision of central bankers.

Several qualifications are needed for effective policy formulation and implementation. One essential requirement is an understanding of our economy and of central banking. Central bank policy is designed to influence economic conditions. Consequently, policymakers need to know in addition to central banking the workings of the economy they are trying to influence. A second quality needed is plenty of courage. Frequently, a central bank needs to take action that is unpopular. Regardless of the policy pursued, Federal Reserve authorities will be criticized. If the policy is one of ease, some will want it easier; others will want it tighter. Moreover, the burden of responsibility makes for timidity; it invites delay and even inaction.

Perhaps the most important quality is an open mind and willingness to innovate. It is easy to get into an intellectual rut and to become an arch defender of doing things in the traditional way. But progress has come, not from rigidity, dogmatism, or sticking to tradition; it has come from intellectual curiosity and a readiness to devise techniques to deal with new problems.

The present Chairman of the Board of Governors recently emphasized the importance of personnel in contrast to form of organization:

> *In the last analysis, whether an institution renders good or bad public service will always depend more upon the character of the human beings engaged in its operations than upon its organizational form and structure.*[1]

Leaders of ability, motivated by devotion to the public interest are the best assurance that the Federal Reserve System will perform a valuable public service in the next fifty years.

---

[1] U.S. Congress, *The Federal Reserve System After Fifty Years*, Hearings, Subcommittee on Domestic Finance, Committee on Banking and Currency, House of Representatives, 88th Cong., 2d Sess. (Washington: U.S. Government Printing Office, 1964), pp. 16–17.

APPENDIX

LIST OF POLICYMAKERS
FEDERAL RESERVE SYSTEM,
1914-1964

MEMBERS OF THE BOARD OF GOVERNORS, 1914-1964[a]

APPOINTIVE MEMBERS

Name	Term of office[b]
Charles S. Hamlin	Aug. 10, 1914–Feb. 3, 1936
Paul M. Warburg	Aug. 10, 1914–Aug. 9, 1918
Frederic A. Delano	Aug. 10, 1914–July 21, 1918
W. P. G. Harding	Aug. 10, 1914–Aug. 9, 1922
Adolph C. Miller	Aug. 10, 1914–Feb. 3, 1936
Albert Strauss	Oct. 26, 1918–Mar. 15, 1920
Henry A. Moehlenpah	Nov. 10, 1919–Aug. 9, 1920
Edmund Platt	June 8, 1920–Sept. 14, 1930
David C. Wills	Sept. 29, 1920–Mar. 4, 1921
John R. Mitchell	May 12, 1921–May 12, 1923
Milo D. Campbell	Mar. 14, 1923–Mar. 22, 1923
Daniel R. Crissinger	May 1, 1923–Sept. 15, 1927
George R. James	May 14, 1923–Feb. 3, 1936
Edward H. Cunningham	May 14, 1923–Nov. 28, 1930
Roy A. Young	Oct. 4, 1927–Aug. 31, 1930
Eugene Meyer	Sept. 16, 1930–May 10, 1933
Wayland W. Magee	May 18, 1931–Jan. 24, 1933
Eugene R. Black	May 19, 1933–Aug. 15, 1934
M. S. Szymczak	June 14, 1933–May 31, 1961
J. J. Thomas	June 14, 1933–Feb. 10, 1936
Marriner S. Eccles	Nov. 15, 1934–July 14, 1951
Joseph A. Broderick	Feb. 3, 1936–Sept. 30, 1937
John K. McKee	Feb. 3, 1936–Apr. 4, 1946
Ronald Ransom	Feb. 3, 1936–Dec. 2, 1947
Ralph W. Morrison	Feb. 10, 1936–July 9, 1936
Chester C. Davis	June 25, 1936–Apr. 15, 1941
Ernest G. Draper	Mar. 30, 1938–Sept. 1, 1950
Rudolph M. Evans	Mar. 14, 1942–Aug. 13, 1954
James K. Vardaman, Jr.	Apr. 4, 1946–Nov. 30, 1958
Lawrence Clayton	Feb. 14, 1947–Dec. 4, 1949
Thomas B. McCabe	Apr. 15, 1948–Mar. 31, 1951
Edward L. Norton	Sept. 1, 1950–Feb. 1, 1952
Oliver S. Powell	Sept. 1, 1950–June 30, 1952

184

Name	Term of office[b]
Wm. McC. Martin, Jr.	Apr. 2, 1951–
A. L. Mills, Jr.	Feb. 18, 1952–Mar. 1, 1965
J. L. Robertson	Feb. 18, 1952–
Paul E. Miller	Aug. 13, 1954–Oct. 21, 1954
C. Canby Balderston	Aug. 12, 1954–
Charles N. Shepardson	Mar. 17, 1955–
G. H. King, Jr.	Mar. 25, 1959–Sept. 18, 1963
George W. Mitchell	Aug. 31, 1961–
J. Dewey Daane	Nov. 29, 1963–
Sherman J. Maisel	Apr. 30, 1965–

CHAIRMEN[c]

Charles S. Hamlin	Aug. 10, 1914–Aug. 9, 1916
W. P. G. Harding	Aug. 10, 1916–Aug. 9, 1922
Daniel R. Crissinger	May 1, 1923–Sept. 15, 1927
Roy A. Young	Oct. 4, 1927–Aug. 31, 1930
Eugene Meyer	Sept. 16, 1930–May 10, 1933
Eugene R. Black	May 19, 1933–Aug. 15, 1934
Marriner S. Eccles	Nov. 15, 1934–Jan. 31, 1948
Thomas B. McCabe	Apr. 15, 1948–Mar. 31, 1951
Wm. McC. Martin, Jr.	Apr. 2, 1951–

VICE CHAIRMEN[c]

Frederic A. Delano	Aug. 10, 1914–Aug. 9, 1916
Paul M. Warburg	Aug. 10, 1916–Aug. 9, 1918
Albert Strauss	Oct. 26, 1918–Mar. 15, 1920
Edmund Platt	July 23, 1920–Sept. 14, 1930
J. J. Thomas	Aug. 21, 1934–Feb. 10, 1936
Ronald Ransom	Aug. 6, 1936–Dec. 2, 1947
C. Canby Balderston	Mar. 11, 1955–

EX OFFICIO MEMBERS[a]

SECRETARIES OF THE TREASURY

W. G. McAdoo	Dec. 23, 1913–Dec. 15, 1918
Carter Glass	Dec. 16, 1918–Feb. 1, 1920
David F. Houston	Feb. 2, 1920–Mar. 3, 1921
Andrew W. Mellon	Mar. 4, 1921–Feb. 12, 1932
Ogden L. Mills	Feb. 12, 1932–Mar. 4, 1933
William H. Woodin	Mar. 4, 1933–Dec. 31, 1933
Henry Morgenthau, Jr.	Jan. 1, 1934–Feb. 1, 1936

Name   Term of office[b]

COMPTROLLERS OF THE CURRENCY

John Skelton Williams	Feb. 2, 1914–Mar. 2, 1921
Daniel R. Crissinger	Mar. 17, 1921–Apr. 30, 1923
Henry M. Dawes	May 1, 1923–Dec. 17, 1924
Joseph W. McIntosh	Dec. 20, 1924–Nov. 20, 1928
J. W. Pole	Nov. 21, 1928–Sept. 20, 1932
J. F. T. O'Connor	May 11, 1933–Feb. 1, 1936

PRESIDENTS OF FEDERAL RESERVE BANKS, 1914-1964[d]

Name   Term of office

BOSTON

Alfred L. Aiken	Nov. 25, 1914–Dec. 20, 1917
Charles A. Morss	Dec. 20, 1917–Dec. 31, 1922
W. P. G. Harding	Jan. 16, 1923–Apr. 7, 1930
Roy A. Young	Sept. 1, 1930–Mar. 31, 1942
W. W. Paddock	Apr. 1, 1942–May 1, 1944
Ralph E. Flanders	May 1, 1944–Feb. 28, 1946
Laurence F. Whittemore	Mar. 1, 1946–Oct. 4, 1948
Joseph A. Erickson	Dec. 15, 1948–Feb. 28, 1961
George H. Ellis	Mar. 1, 1961–

NEW YORK

Benjamin Strong, Jr.	Oct. 5, 1914–Oct. 16, 1928
George L. Harrison	Nov. 22, 1928–Dec. 31, 1940
Allan Sproul	Jan. 1, 1941–June 30, 1956
Alfred Hayes	Aug. 1, 1956–

PHILADELPHIA

Charles J. Rhoads	Nov. 25, 1914–Feb. 8, 1918
E. P. Passmore	Feb. 8, 1918–Feb. 28, 1920
George W. Norris	Apr. 5, 1920–Feb. 29, 1936
J. S. Sinclair	Mar. 13, 1936–June 30, 1941
Alfred H. Williams	July 1, 1941–Feb. 28, 1958
Karl R. Bopp	Mar. 1, 1958–

Name	Term of office

CLEVELAND

E. R. Fancher	Nov. 2, 1914–Jan. 16, 1935
M. J. Fleming	Jan. 19, 1935–Sept. 15, 1944
Ray M. Gidney	Nov. 1, 1944–Apr. 16, 1953
Wilbur D. Fulton	May 14, 1953–Apr. 30, 1963
W. Braddock Hickman	May 1, 1963–

RICHMOND

George J. Seay	Oct. 5, 1914–Feb. 29, 1936
Hugh Leach	Mar. 12, 1936–Feb. 28, 1961
Edward A. Wayne	Mar. 1, 1961–

ATLANTA

Joseph A. McCord	Nov. 16, 1914–Mar. 1, 1919
M. B. Wellborn	Mar. 1, 1919–Dec. 31, 1927
Eugene R. Black	{ Jan. 13, 1928–May 18, 1933 { Aug. 16, 1934–Dec. 19, 1934
Oscar Newton	Jan. 15, 1935–Feb. 13, 1939
Robert S. Parker	Feb. 20, 1939–Mar. 28, 1941
W. S. McLarin, Jr.	May 9, 1941–Mar. 1, 1951
Malcolm Bryan	Apr. 1, 1951–

CHICAGO

James B. McDougal	Nov. 25, 1914–Mar. 1, 1934
G. J. Schaller	Mar. 2, 1934–Mar. 1, 1941
C. S. Young	Mar. 1, 1941–Mar. 1, 1956
Carl E. Allen, Jr.	Oct. 1, 1956–Dec. 31, 1961
Charles J. Scanlon	Jan. 4, 1962–

ST. LOUIS

Rolla Wells	Oct. 28, 1914–Feb. 5, 1919
David C. Biggs	Feb. 5, 1919–Dec. 31, 1928
Wm. McC. Martin	Jan. 16, 1929–Mar. 1, 1941
Chester C. Davis	Apr. 16, 1941–Feb. 1, 1951
Delos C. Johns	Feb. 1, 1951–Feb. 28, 1962
Harry A. Shuford	Oct. 1, 1962–

Name	Term of office

MINNEAPOLIS

Name	Term of office
Theodore Wold	Oct. 14, 1914–Oct. 1, 1919
R. A. Young	Oct. 1, 1919–Sept. 26, 1927
W. B. Geery	Oct. 3, 1927–Mar. 1, 1936
J. N. Peyton	Mar. 1, 1936–June 30, 1952
O. S. Powell	July 1, 1952–Mar. 31, 1957
Frederick L. Deming	Apr. 1, 1957–Feb. 1, 1965
Hugh D. Galusha, Jr.	May 1, 1965–

KANSAS CITY

Name	Term of office
Charles M. Sawyer	Oct. 17, 1914–Dec. 31, 1915
J. Z. Miller, Jr.	Jan. 1, 1916–July 1, 1922
W. J. Bailey	July 1, 1922–Dec. 31, 1931
George H. Hamilton	Jan. 7, 1932–Mar. 1, 1941
H. G. Leedy	Aug. 28, 1941–Feb. 28, 1961
George H. Clay	Mar. 1, 1961–

DALLAS

Name	Term of office
Oscar Wells	Nov. 2, 1914–Feb. 24, 1915
R. L. Van Zandt	Feb. 24, 1915–Jan. 7, 1922
B. A. McKinney	Jan. 16, 1922–May 16, 1925
Lynn P. Talley	July 1, 1925–Oct. 1, 1931
B. A. McKinney	Oct. 5, 1931–Apr. 2, 1939
R. R. Gilbert	Apr. 13, 1939–Sept. 1, 1953
Watrous H. Irons	Feb. 15, 1954–

SAN FRANCISCO

Name	Term of office
Archibald Kains	Nov. 25, 1914–July 5, 1917
James K. Lynch	Aug. 7, 1917–Apr. 28, 1919
John U. Calkins	May 16, 1919–Feb. 29, 1936
Wm. A. Day	Apr. 1, 1936–Dec. 31, 1945
Ira Clerk	Jan. 1, 1946–Sept. 28, 1946
C. E. Earhart	Oct. 17, 1946–Mar. 1, 1956
H. N. Mangels	Mar. 1, 1956–Feb. 28, 1961
Eliot J. Swan	Mar. 1, 1961–

CHAIRMEN AND FEDERAL RESERVE AGENTS OF THE FEDERAL RESERVE BANKS, 1914-1936 ͤ

Name	Term of office
BOSTON	
Frederic H. Curtiss	Oct. 1, 1914–Mar. 1, 1936
NEW YORK	
Pierre Jay	Sept. 30, 1914–Dec. 31, 1926
Gates W. McGarrah	May 1, 1927–Feb. 27, 1930
J. Herbert Case	Feb. 28, 1930–Mar. 1, 1936
PHILADELPHIA	
Richard L. Austin	Oct. 8, 1914–Mar. 1, 1936
CLEVELAND	
D. C. Wills	Oct. 8, 1914–Sept. 30, 1920
Lewis B. Williams	Sept. 30, 1920–Mar. 4, 1921
D. C. Wills	Mar. 5, 1921–Oct. 22, 1925
George DeCamp	Dec. 19, 1925–Mar. 15, 1933
Lewis B. Williams	Mar. 15, 1933–Nov. 27, 1934
Wm. H. Fletcher	Jan. 1, 1935–Mar. 1, 1936
RICHMOND	
William Ingle	Oct. 5, 1914–Feb. 12, 1916
Caldwell Hardy	Apr. 1, 1916–Aug. 26, 1923
Wm. W. Hoxton	Sept. 15, 1923–Dec. 20, 1935 ᶠ
ATLANTA	
M. B. Wellborn	Oct. 16, 1914–Feb. 28, 1919
Joseph A. McCord	Mar. 1, 1919–Dec. 31, 1924
Oscar Newton	Jan. 1, 1925–Jan. 15, 1935 ᶠ

189

Name	Term of office

CHICAGO

Charles H. Bosworth	Nov. 16, 1914–Dec. 31, 1916
William A. Heath	Jan. 1, 1917–Dec. 31, 1930
Eugene M. Stevens	Jan. 1, 1931–Mar. 31, 1936

ST. LOUIS

William McC. Martin	Oct. 28, 1914–Jan. 16, 1929
Rolla Wells	Jan. 23, 1929–May 6, 1930
John S. Wood	May 9, 1930–Mar. 1, 1936

MINNEAPOLIS

John H. Rich	Oct. 1, 1914–May 20, 1924
John R. Mitchell	Sept. 8, 1924–Jan. 31, 1933
J. N. Peyton	May 15, 1933–Feb. 29, 1936

KANSAS CITY

J. Z. Miller, Jr.	Oct. 16, 1914–Jan. 5, 1916
Charles M. Sawyer	Jan. 10, 1916–Dec. 31, 1917
Asa E. Ramsay	Jan. 1, 1918–May 1, 1923
M. L. McClure	May 1, 1923–Dec. 5, 1934ᵍ
J. J. Thomas	Feb. 10, 1936–Mar. 1, 1936

DALLAS

E. O. Tenison	Nov. 16, 1914–Jan. 15, 1916
Wm. F. Ramsey	Jan. 15, 1916–Oct. 27, 1922
W. B. Newsome	Nov. 3, 1922–Mar. 15, 1923
Lynn P. Talley	Mar. 15, 1923–June 30, 1925
C. C. Walsh	July 1, 1925–Mar. 1, 1936

SAN FRANCISCO

John Perrin	Oct. 13, 1914–Mar. 1, 1926
Isaac B. Newton	Mar. 1, 1926–June 22, 1934ᶠ

ᵃ Under the provisions of the original Federal Reserve Act the Federal Reserve Board was composed of seven members, including five members appointed by the President and two ex officio members—the Secretary of the Treasury, who was Chairman of the Board, and the Comptroller of the Currency. The original term of office was 10 years, and the five original appointive members had terms of 2, 4, 6, 8, and 10 years, respectively. In 1922 the number of appointive members was increased to six, and in 1933 the term of office was increased to 12 years. The Banking Act of 1935, approved Aug. 23, 1935, changed the name of the Federal Reserve Board to the Board of Governors of the Federal Reserve System and provided that the Board should be composed of seven appointive members; that the Secretary of the Treasury and the Comptroller of the Currency should continue to serve as members until Feb. 1, 1936; that the appointive members in office on the date of that Act should continue to serve until Feb. 1, 1936, or until their successors were appointed and had qualified; and that thereafter the terms of members should be 14 years and that the designation of Chairman and Vice Chairman of the Board should be for a term of four years. Source: Board of Governors.

ᵇ Beginning of term represents effective date of appointment.

ᶜ Chairman and Vice Chairman were designated Governor and Vice Governor before Aug. 23, 1935.

ᵈ Source: Official records. There were some discrepancies in earlier years as to date the term of office began, apparently reflecting difference between announcement and effective date; effective dates have been used when available.

ᵉ Source: Official records. There were some discrepancies in earlier years as to date the term of office began, apparently reflecting differences between announcement and effective date of appointment. Effective date of appointment used whenever available. The Banking Act of 1935 changed the duties and responsibilities of the Chairman and Federal Reserve Agent. Effective March 1, 1936, the position ceased to be one in which the official devoted his full time to the Reserve Bank.

ᶠ Appointment of successor not effective prior to March 1, 1936.

ᵍ Position vacant from December 5, 1934 to February 10, 1936.

INDEX

INDEX